Amulet Obsession

Picturesque Beaded Purse Patterns

Written & Illustrated by

Barbara E. Elbe

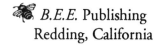 B.E.E. Publishing
Redding, California

Amulet Obsession
Picturesque Beaded Purse Patterns

By Barbara E. Elbe

Published by:

🐝 **B.E.E. Publishing**
556 Hanland Court
Redding, CA 96003

First Printing: June 1998

Elbe, Barbara E.
    Amulet obsession : picturesque beaded purse patterns / by Barbara E. Elbe -- 1st ed.

    ISBN 0-9653622-2-1

    Library of Congress Catalog Number: 98-92548

Table of Contents

Table of Contents

Introduction

Open fields on a hot summers' day, cool winter evenings in the snow, ocean surf crashing against the rocks. These are just a few of the ideas that influenced the purses included in **Amulet Obsession**. Titled appropriately, and including 17 inspirational designs, I hope this will be a difficult book to put down.

The first chapter includes ten purses using Horizontal Brick Stitch done in a tubular fashion. Continuing where **Back to Beadin'** left off, there are birds in flight over fields and marshes, Cardinals patiently waiting out a snow storm in the branches of a barren winter tree and a California Quail alone in a warm autumn field. Other designs included in this chapter are, Girl by the Sea on a hazy summer day and a White Tailed Deer in a snowy winter forest.

All Horizontal Brick Stitch patterns can be converted to Flat Peyote Stitch. To do this, follow the pattern vertically instead of horizontally, as shown in this book. Then close the two ends together with peyote stitch to form a tube. Stitch the bottom closed.

The next chapter has two unique designs using Vertical Brick Stitch. One is of Ol' Saint Nicholas clothed in a long red robe. He is carrying a sack of presents over one shoulder and a small Christmas tree in his other hand. All done on a blue iris background trimmed with 22 karat gold. The other is of Merlin the Magician with a very bushy, three dimensional beard made using stick fringe.

Vertical Brick Stitch is the easiest to convert to flat peyote. It can also be converted to tubular peyote with the addition of a bottom.

The last chapter of designs, which features five purses, introduces Square Stitch. One piece is sculptured in shape. This is the beautiful Lady Guinevere with long golden hair and enchanting big blue eyes. Just the top edge of her lacy white gown shows, adorned along the bottom edge with topaz crystal. Another is an exotic Peacock with the fringe used as it's tail, including gold filled and crystal beads for added sparkle.

Square Stitch can easily be used for loom work, following pattern exactly as shown.

The different straps featured with the purses shown are completely illustrated and explained. The Spiral Rope strap has been introduced, adding elegance to the purses. It may look difficult, but is quite easy to learn and fairly fast to complete.

Delica beads are now featured in over 500 colors. Although they are not quite as easy as mixing colors on an artists palette, the large selection to choose from does allow for scenes to be created like the ones included in this book.

I hope you will become "Obsessed" by the enjoyment of making these miniature amulet purses as much as I did designing them.

On a personal note...

It has been a pleasure meeting and talking to other beaders by phone, over the Internet and through the wonderful letters I have received. Until Back to Beadin' was self published, I had no idea there were so many beaders out there.

It is a comfort to know we have so many things in common --

Our spilling of beads all over the area we work and into the depths of the carpet below, never to be found again --

Our abandoning of household chores for the sake of "one more row" to bead --

Our love for those shinny little pieces of glass, which are such a joy to behold and fun to run our fingers through --

Our total dedication to the ever evolving craft of beading.

Barbara

556 Hanland Court
Redding, CA 96003
(530) 244-0317
fax (530) 244-2336

BeadImages@aol.com
http://members.aol.com/beadimages

Basic Supplies

The most important ingredient in beading is the bead. First you have to decide what type and size of bead you wish to use for a project. In this book, Delica beads are used exclusively.

Delica/Antique These are fairly new to the United States. Delica (DB) are imported from Japan where they are produced by Miyuki Shoji Co., Ltd. There is also another brand called Antique by Toho. They are very much alike and come in many similar colors. Last count, DB had approximately 500 colors to choose from. They are consistent in size and have very large holes, quite unlike seed beads. They are a little smaller than 11/o seed beads, more the size of 12/o but taller. They have also been called Japanese cylinder beads, probably because of their shape.

DB beads can usually be purchased in either 5 to 10 gram packages, or 4 to 8 gram tubes. Wholesale places sell in bulk, 100 gram to kilo packs (1000g). These beads are expensive but well worth it.

Hexagon Another cylinder shaped bead, smaller than DB beads with thinner walls. They are about the size of the 14/o seed bead but taller. Although they are fairly consistent, they are not as good as DB but better than seed. Hexagon (HEX) are easier to find in stores but do not have as good a color selection. Many of these beads come in the hexagon shape (six sided) which gives them an extra shine. If HEX beads are substituted, the purse and design will be much smaller, longer and narrower.

HEX beads are usually sold in the same quantities as the DB beads, but less expensive. Some opaque colors come in hanks. These beads are a worthwhile addition; although they are not used in this book.

Seed These beads have been around for a long time. They come in a variety of sizes: 9/o, largest to 16/o, smallest. There are smaller seed beads, 18/o to 22/o, but these are hard to find and if acquired, they are so tiny a magnifying light is needed to work with them. Colors also become more limited in the smaller beads. The most popular size and available in an almost unlimited variety of colors is 11/o. If size 11/o seed beads are substituted, the purse and design will be much larger. The size 14/o seed bead is much closer to the Delica bead size.

Seed beads usually come in hanks but are sometimes sold by the gram in packs or tubes. They are the least expensive of the three types listed. Most seed beads come from Czechoslovakia. Japan is now importing some very nice colors with larger holes.

Needles It is important to buy needles that are made especially for beading. They are very thin and flexible, perfect for those tiny holes. Do not use regular sewing needles.

Beading needles come in a range of sizes, from very thin size 16, to thicker size 12. The higher the number the thinner the needle. Size 12 works best with DB, HEX and most of the 11/o seed beads. Have a few thinner size 15 needles around for the times your size 12 won't go through the beads.

Depending on how many passes are made with the thread through a bead effects the size of the needle used. Never force a needle through. The bead can break and ruin the piece being worked. It can be annoying having to change to a thinner needle in the middle of a project, but having a bead break can be far worse.

The long Delica Beading Needles would also be a nice addition to your beading supplies. It comes in three sizes: 1 3/4 inches, 3 5/8 inches and 2 inches long The 3 5/8 inch needle seems to be the most useful of the three. It works well for fringe and straps. It is extremely easy to handle and, best of all, easy to thread.

Thread Do not use regular sewing thread. The most common and most available thread used for beading is Nymo®, found in most craft stores in black or white. Colors are a little harder to find. It is a strong, multi-fiber nylon thread.

- A permanent color marking pen works well for coloring white thread. Either color the threads that show on the outer edge, or color the whole section of thread before using by running the thread over the side part of the felt tip pen.

There are a variety of thicknesses to choose from. They range from 000 to 0 (thin to thicker) and A, B and D. A is the thinnest of this group, B is about the same as 0 and D being thickest. I prefer to use 0 for most of the earrings and smaller jewelry, and D for purses, necklaces and bracelets, as it adds strength and rigidity. They can be purchased in two sizes. Most easily found is the bobbin size with approximately 64 - 160 yards (depending on the thickness of thread), and the large 3 ounce cone size, which only comes in black or white. If you do a lot of beading or loom work, the 3 oz. cone is very useful.

- Bobbin size thread has a tendency to curl easier than spool thread. Wetting and stretching it before it is waxed will help to alleviate some of this problem.

- Waxing the thread also helps to make it more manageable. With a cube of beeswax, run the section of thread to be used over the top between thumb and wax. Repeat this 2-3 times.

- Thread Heaven®, a synthetic, is another thread conditioner that can be used in place of beeswax. It comes in a small plastic container, costs more but is long lasting.

- To remove small knots in the thread, use one needle to pierce the center of the knot and another needle to pull the knot apart.

Sylamide® is another thread used by many beaders. It is made up of two strands of nylon twisted and pre-waxed. It comes in a number of colors on spools similar to regular sewing thread and costs a little more than Nymo. Choosing a type of thread comes from experience in working with them. Both Nymo and Sylamide are very strong and work well for beading.

Twist Fringe

This is one of the prettiest fringe and, with practice, not difficult to do. It is hard to explain how many twists work because it is near impossible to count twists that are done by rolling the thread between the thumb and fingers.

I have never had the twists fall out. Once they are pulled into place, they should stay. If you over twist (where the whole strand gets overly ridged from too many twists) it actually seems to be less twisted when pulled into place. Almost like the thread is over stressed.

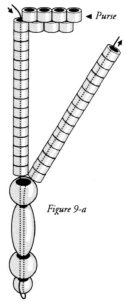

Figure 9-a

1. First string number of DB beads listed along top of illustration along with trim beads. Go back up through the trim, then add the rest of the DB. Make sure the DB beads are of equal length. Even with the same count of beads, they do not always come out even because of inconsistencies. *Figure 9-a*

2. With the purse and fringe laying on the table, pull the thread straight up toward you.

3. With thumb and forefinger right next to the end of the DB beads, start twisting (rolling thread between your thumb and forefinger). The trim beads should spin around to disburse twists to the rest of strand. *Figure 9-b*

4. It is important to hold these twists in place with one hand, and run the twists off the other end of the thread with the needle using your other hand. This helps prevent tangling.

5. Repeat instruction #3 several times. You will know the twisting is working when you hold the two halves next to each other and they twist together.

6. Do not let go of your hold at the top of the DB beads, this is holding the twists in the beaded section of the thread. While holding with one hand, run the needle up the second bead over to the right along the bottom of the purse with your other hand. Pull the fringe into place and adjust fringe.

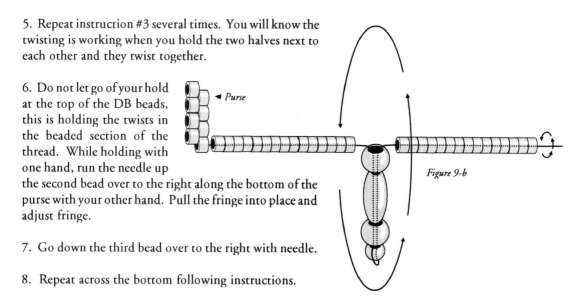

Figure 9-b

7. Go down the third bead over to the right with needle.

8. Repeat across the bottom following instructions.

Stick Fringe

Stick fringe makes a very nice front or accent fringe. It is easy to do, but does take time and a considerable amount of thread. Follow example at right, starting at white arrow add fifteen beads. *Figure 10-a*

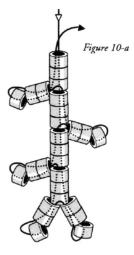

Figure 10-a

1. Go around last bead, up through five. This leaves three beads for bottom branch and puts you in position for next branch.

2. Add three beads, go around last one, up through the two remaining and the three on the main section. This gives a branch off the main section and puts you in position for the next branch.

3. Repeat this to the top. The amount of beads on each branch, or between each branch, can vary. Follow illustration shown with each design.

24" Peyote Style Strap

There are a number of variations that can be done with this style. They all use the same principles. Follow illustration shown with each design. String in order (e.g.) sections A, B, C (center), B & A in reverse to finish strap. Some straps will actually have the center marked. Others show a break in the beads and an number to the left. This is not the center of the strap. Go by the number of beads listed, not the illustration.

1. Attach two waxed 40 inch sections of thread, unless otherwise stated, to the upper corners of purse where shown. Weave ends of thread into purse approximately one third of way down to secure.

2. Pick up amount of DB beads needed for peyote section of the strap with first needle and thread. The total beads per section is listed with each individual illustration. It is best to have a needle on the end of each thread.

3. With second needle and thread, go through first DB on first strand, pick up one DB bead, go through next, pick up another, go through next. Repeat until total needed.

4. To achieve an even distribution of thread, slide the DB beads on thread until they are about 1/2" from where they should be. *Figure 10-b*

5. Now, row by row slide them back into position. *Figure 10-c*

   • Do small sections at a time. If an error is found, there will be less to take out.

6. Attach to other corner of the purse where shown. Weave ends in, cut.

Figure 10-b & 10-c

Spiral Rope Strap

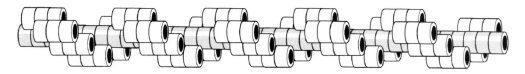

Shown to me by a fellow beader, I found the spiral rope both elegant and easy to do. This technique requires a large amount of thread and beads with larger holes. If at all possible, the strap should be completed in one section of thread for strength. This can be achieved in one of two ways. One is to do the strap in two sections and use a clasp to connect. The other way, which is done in this book, is to start beading the strap in the middle of the long section of thread, work one direction to the end, then the other. This way you only have to deal with one half the length of thread at a time. It may help to wind the unused half of thread onto something to keep it out of the way. Make sure to leave at least 12 inches of thread at each end for dangles and attaching to the purse.

The straps in the book are 26.5 to 32 inches in length. Using DB beads, it takes approximately 10 inches of thread per inch of strap. Consider you will be working with up to a 10 yard section.

Starting in the middle of a long waxed section of thread, add the four beads that will make up the core of the strap and the three beads that will be the outer spiraling beads. *Figure 11-a*

Starting at white arrow, go back up through all seven beads as shown in *Figure 11-b*. Pull the three beads next to other four as shown, and run needle up through the four core beads. *Figure 11-c*

Figure 11-a

Figure 11-b

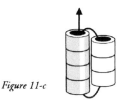

Figure 11-c

Add one core bead and three outer beads.
Figure 12-a

Go up through the three core beads as shown in
Figure 12-b. Pull into place.

Figure 12-a   Figure 12-b

Go down through the single core bead shown in
Figure 12-c. That bead will flip into place over the
top of the other core beads.   *Figure 12-d*

Repeat from *Figure 12-a* thorough *Figure 12-d*
until desired length.

- To create an even spiral, make sure to
  position each three bead spiral group after
  previous one, not accidentally between.

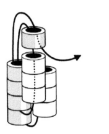

Figure 12-c   Figure 12-d

Horizontal Brick Stitch
Instructions & Patterns

Tubular Horizontal Brick Stitch

1. Cut a section of size D White Nymo® thread 5 yards long, wax.

    - White size D Nymo thread is used in this book unless otherwise stated.

2. Place needle just 2-3 inches in from the end.

    - Size D thread is thick making it hard to slide the needle. Having it close to the end makes it easier to take the needle on and off.

    - The needle cuts into the thread causing it to fray. With the needle so close to the end, the damage is in an area that will not be used for the purse.

    - Run fingers down the thread occasionally, dangling the needle and thread in the air to get the twirls in the thread out. This helps to keep the thread from tangling.

    - It is very important when stitching the beads together to keep the tension loose. Pull the beads into place gently. This will produce an end product that is flexible. Just keep telling yourself, "relax".

    - Re-wax the thread occasionally.

3. Pick up two beads, place 2 1/2 yards in (halfway point on thread). This allows half the thread for the upper section of the pattern, and the other half to begin lower section. *Figure 13-a*

4. Start with the base row. All base rows, including the top 6 rows, are worked from left to right. The lower section of the purse is worked from right to left, going around the back to the front.

    - All base rows are marked with *. On all the purses done in brick stitch, the base row is started on the 6th row down from the top. In the vertical designs the base row is started in the middle of the purse. There are two reasons for this.

Figure 13-a

- When constructing the base row, you will find it does not lay even. To solve this problem I have found if you bead both directions, above and below, this helps.

- By starting further down in the purse (or in the middle, as in the vertical designs) a longer section of thread can be utilized. Start with a 5 yard section, divide it in half, use 2 1/2 yards for the base row, the rows above and the lace finish. The remaining 2 1/2 yards allows for another 7-eight rows to be added the other direction without having to add a new section of thread.

5. Hold the two beads in place with your thumb and forefinger, loop around with the needle and pass through the beads again in the same direction. *Figure 14-a* Pull together, side by side. *Figure 14-b*

Figure 14-a   *Figure 14-b*

6. Add to the base row until you have the amount of beads stated in the pattern. *Figure 14-c* Connect ends together (starting at white arrow) and pull together snug. *Figure 14-d*

Figure 14-c   *Figure 14-d*

ROW TWO Pick up two beads following design being worked on and attach as you would one bead. *Figure 14-e* Continue around design (working left to right).

7. Join ends together by going through the first bead at the beginning of the row and attaching to the loop of the previous row. *Figure 14-f* Continue to top of purse (a total of six rows).

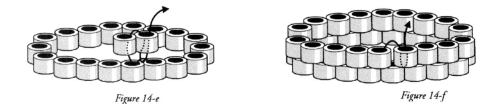

Figure 14-e   *Figure 14-f*

8. Add optional lace along top row. *Figure 15-a or Figure 54-a & b.* To keep thread from showing along the top edge of the purse section where the lace is connected, make the thread loops on inside of purse instead of outside by turning the purse inside out as you would a pillow case.

- Turning the bead work inside out also works if you find the design is facing the opposite direction.
- Once the piece gets too large, turning inside out will not be possible.

9. Attach new 2 1/2 yard sections of thread as needed, weaving end securely into purse. The lower section of the purse is worked from right to left.

- A 2 1/2 yard section of thread is used because it is easy to handle, especially with having the needle only 2-3 inches from the end of the thread.

- Size D thread makes too big a knot to hide properly. Instead of a knot, work the thread back and forth three to four times through three or four beads at a time to hold securely.

- Do not force the needle through too many beads at once when tying off. The last thing you want is a broken bead. Size D thread is too thick to use with a needle much thinner than size 12, so be very careful.

10. Stitch bottom of purse together on Horizontal brick Stitch and Square Stitch. The sides would be stitched together on Vertical Brick Stitch. *Figure 15-b*

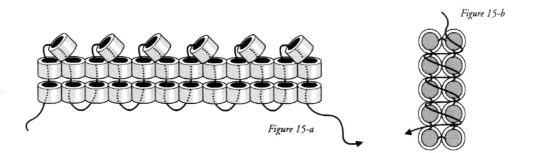

Figure 15-b

Figure 15-a

Iris Bouquet

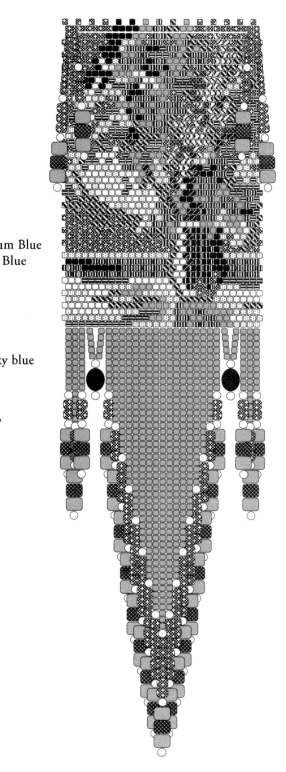

	DB 27	Metallic Teal Iris
	DB 56	Lined Magenta AB
	DB 57	Lined Sky Blue AB
	DB 72	Lined Pale Lilac AB
	DB 80	Lined Pale Lavender AB
	DB 124	Transparent Chartreuse Luster
	DB 201	White Pearl
	DB 233	Lined Crystal/Yellow Luster
	DB 272	Lined Topaz/Yellow AB
	AQ 461	Metallic Violet Iris
	DB 693	Semi-Matte Silver Lined Medium Blue
	DB 905	Lined Crystal Shimmering Sky Blue

* Base Row 58 Beads
    30 - Front Design (Row #6)
    28 - Back done in:
        DB 905 Lined Crystal Shim. Sky blue

Total number of rows in design: 47

Purse total dimensions: 2" x 6 1/8 "
    Bag: 2" x 2 5/8"
    Fringe: 3 1/2"

Iris Bouquet

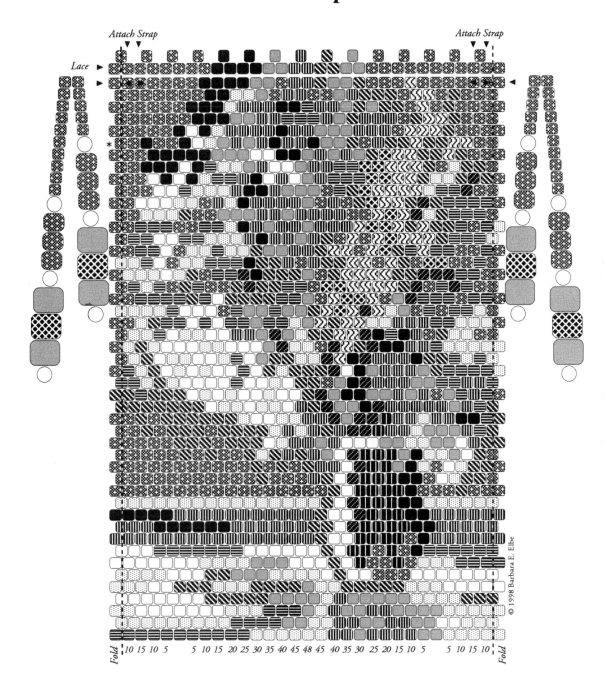

© 1998 Barbara E. Elbe

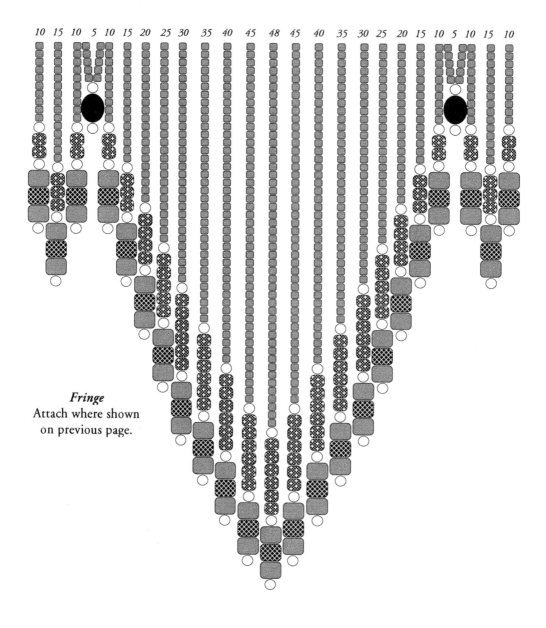

10 15 10 5 10 15 20 25 30 35 40 45 48 45 40 35 30 25 20 15 10 5 10 15 10

Fringe
Attach where shown
on previous page.

Trim Beads

113 -- 2 mm Gold Filled Beads

6 -- 4 mm Blue Iris Fire Polish Crystal

158 -- TD1823 - Size 8/o - Lined Aqua Shimmering Blue Triangle Beads

31 -- TC1166 - Size 5/o - Lined/Gold Mauve AB Triangle Beads

62 -- TC1834 - Size 5/o - Lined Mauve/Fuchsia Triangle Beads

Strap

1. Cut two, 40 inch sections of thread.

2. Run each thread down where marked with arrows shown on the front diagram of the purse, previous page. Pull through approximately 8 inches of thread for the dangle.

3. Add dangle beads. Go around end gold bead, back up through dangle beads and back into the original single bead where started.

4. Run needle back down into purse through three to four beads at a time until about one inch from the top. Weave end in securely and cut.

5. Repeat with other section of strap.

6. Attach needles to the other end of threads and follow illustration at right, along with instructions for 24" Peyote Style Strap, page 10.

7. Repeat 2 through 5 for attaching to other side of purse.

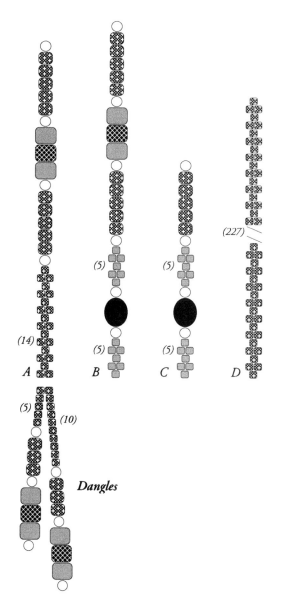

Dangles

Girl by the Sea

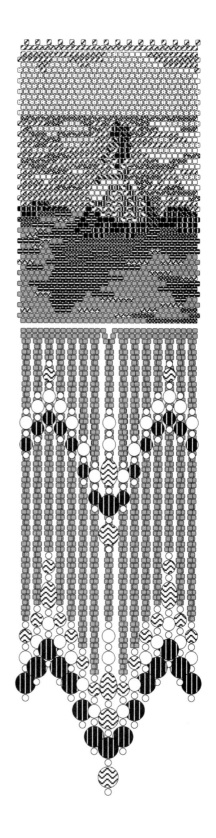

▨	DB 57	Lined Sky Blue AB
◩	DB 67	Lined Flesh AB
◫	DB 70	Lined Rose Pink AB
☐	DB 201	White Pearl
⬚	DB 203	Ceylon Light Yellow
⬯	DB 234	Pale Pink Pearl
■	DB 310	Matte Black
⊠	DB 373	Matte Metallic Leaf Green
⊟	DB 374	Matte Metallic Seafoam Green
▥	DB 769	Matte Transparent Cocoa Brown
▦	DB 771	Matte Translucent Sand
▩	DB 852	Matte Transparent Light Topaz AB
▨	DB 853	Matte Transparent Dark Topaz AB
▤	DB 883	Matte Opaque Cream AB
▩	DB 905	Lined Crystal Shimmering Sky Blue

* Base Row: 62 Beads
    32 - Front Design (Row #6)
    30 - Back done in:
        DB 203 Ceylon Light Yellow

Total number of rows in the design: 51

Purse total dimensions: 2 1/8" x 7 1/8 "
    Bag: 2 1/8" x 2 3/4"
    Fringe: 4 3/8"

Girl by the Sea

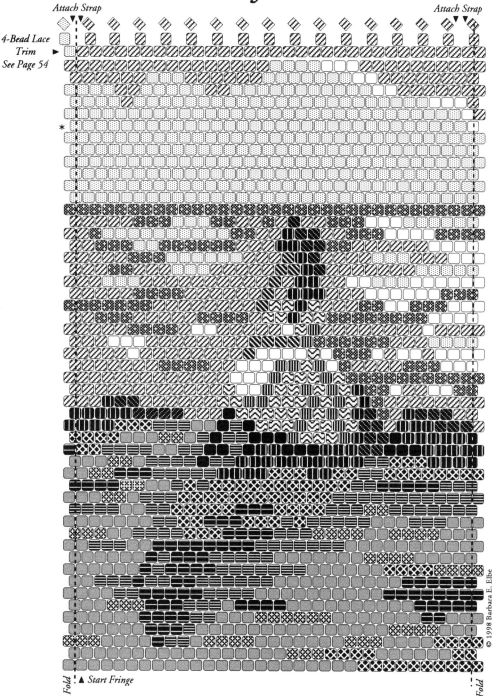

Attach Strap

Attach Strap

4-Bead Lace
Trim
See Page 54 ▶

*

Fold ▲ Start Fringe

Fold

© 1998 Barbara E. Elbe

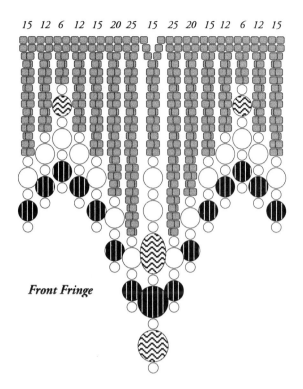

Front Fringe

Trim Beads

○ 179 - 2 mm Gold Filled Beads

🌑 34 - 4 mm Leopard Jasper

○ 52 - 4 mm Mother of Pearl

◍ 24 - 4 mm Light Pink AB Fire Polish Crystal

◍ 8 - 5 x 7 mm Light Pink Fire Polish Crystal

🌑 16 - 6 mm Leopard Jasper

◍ 3 - 6 mm Clear Light Pink AB Druk

22

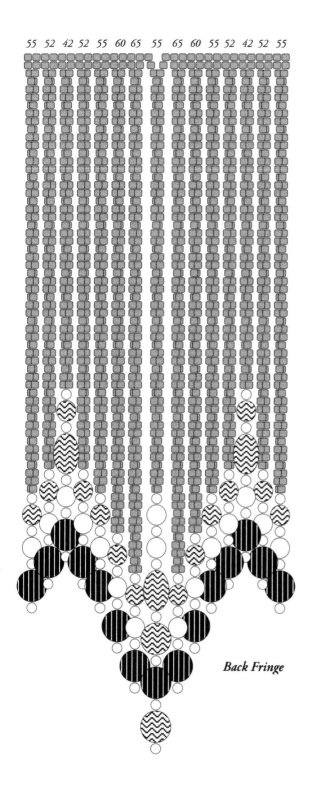

55 52 42 52 55 60 65 55 65 60 55 52 42 52 55

Back Fringe

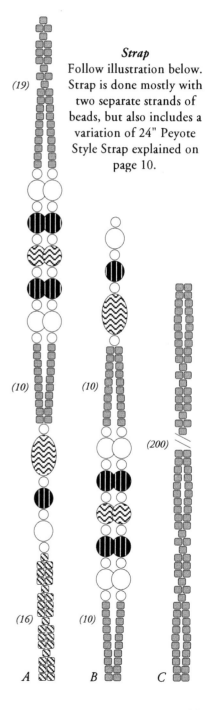

(19)

Strap
Follow illustration below. Strap is done mostly with two separate strands of beads, but also includes a variation of 24" Peyote Style Strap explained on page 10.

(10)   *(10)*

(200)

(16)   *(10)*

A   *B*   *C*

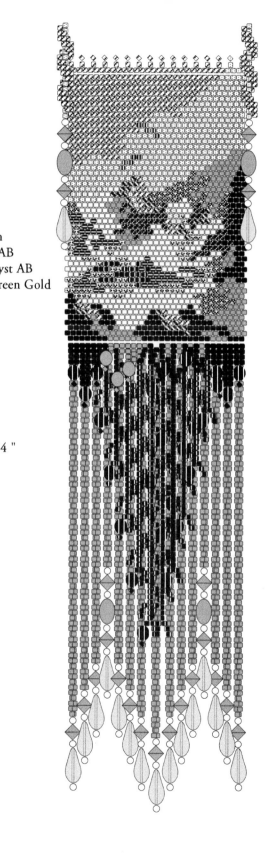

Crashing Surf

▨	DB 54	Lined Peach AB
☰	DB 60	Lined Lime AB
☐	DB 201	White Pearl
▦	DB 233	Lined Crystal Yellow Luster
▨	DB 252	Ceylon Grey
▉	DB 325	Matte Metallic Blue Iris
▥	DB 327	Matte Metallic Teal Iris
▥	DB 351	Matte White
▨	DB 769	Matte Transparent Cocoa Brown
▨	DB 853	Matte Transparent Dark Topaz AB
▨	DB 857	Matte Transparent Light Amethyst AB
▨	DB 903	Lined Crystal Shim. Ultra Lt. Green Gold

* Base Row: 62 Beads
    33 - Front Design (Row #6)
    29 - Back done in:
        DB 54 Lined Peach AB

Total number of rows in design: 50

    Purse total dimensions: 2 1/8" x 7 1/4 "
        Bag: 2 1/8" x 2 7/8"
        Fringe: 4 3/8

Crashing Surf

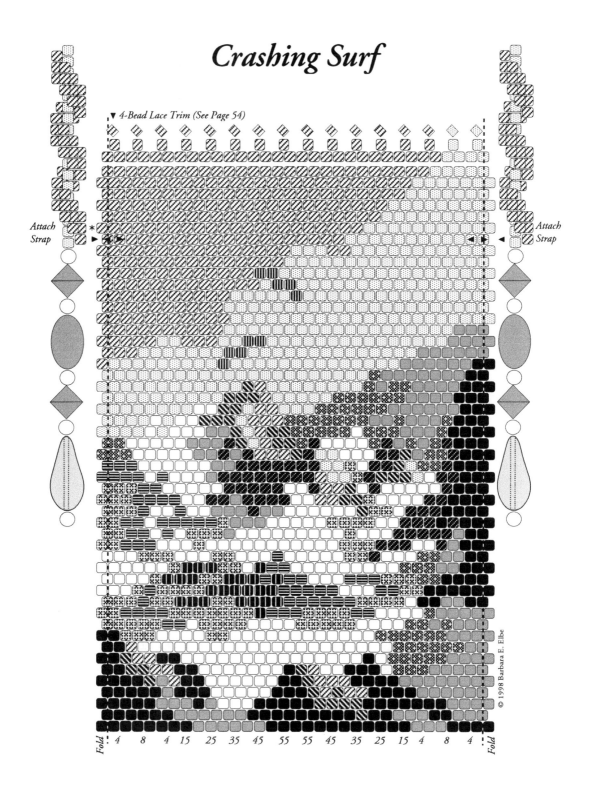

▼ 4-Bead Lace Trim (See Page 54)

Attach Strap

*

Attach Strap

© 1998 Barbara E. Elbe

Fold   4   8   4   15   25   35   45   55   55   45   35   25   15   4   8   4   Fold

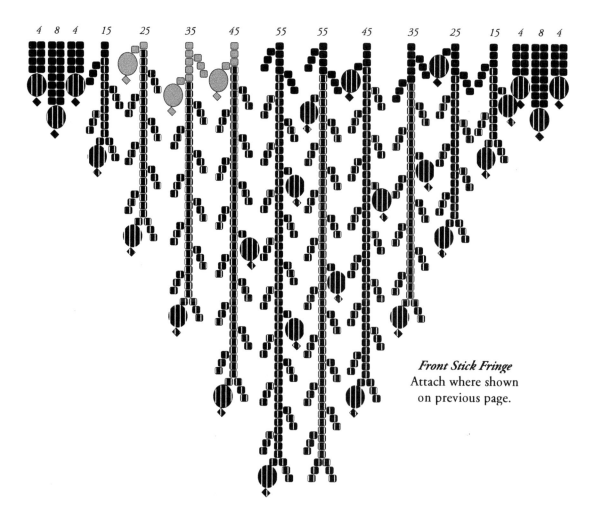

Front Stick Fringe
Attach where shown
on previous page.

Trim Beads

59 --	2 mm Gold Filled Beads
21 --	4 mm Amethyst Austrian Crystal
3 --	4 mm Dark Amethyst AB Fire Polish Crystal
25 --	4 mm Green Iris Fire Polish Crystal
4 --	5 x 7 mm Amethyst Fire Polish Crystal
17 --	6 x 11 mm Amethyst Teardrop

70 65 60 42 60 65 70 75 70 65 60 42 60 65 70

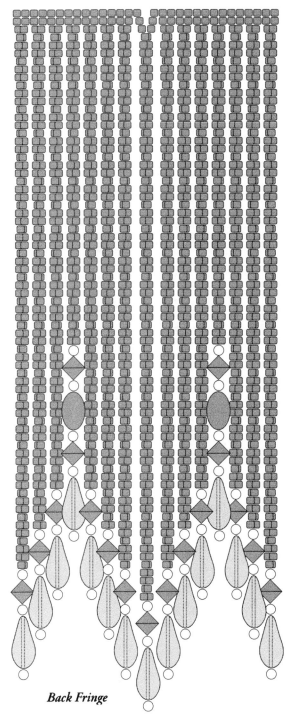

Back Fringe

26 1/2 inches in length without dangle.
Add dangle beads to tail of strap, go around end gold bead and back up through the dangle, first 4 core beads and down the 3 outer spiral beads. You are positioned to attach to purse.

The attachment to horizontal brick stitch is more difficult than attaching to vertical brick stitch or peyote stitch. Below is a general idea of what to do. You may need to make a few adjustments to this.

1. Starting at back left side of purse, attach by first going up beads starting on row 7 and coming out bead directly above on row 5.

2. Next, go down through first set of 3 outer spiral beads.

3. Go back up through same beads on purse, but out row 4 this time.

3. Up through rows 3, 2, and 1 of purse, keeping as straight a line as possible, down through the set of spiral beads that line up best with purse.

4. Up through purse again coming out row 1 again.

5. Attach strap to front in same way. Go down rows 1, 2, and 3 starting at next bead over from where last exited.

6. Up a set of spiral beads, down beads in purse again but this time coming out row 7 in as straight a line as possible.

7. Up through spiral beads and back into purse.

8. Weave tail into purse securely, cut.

27

Field of Flowers

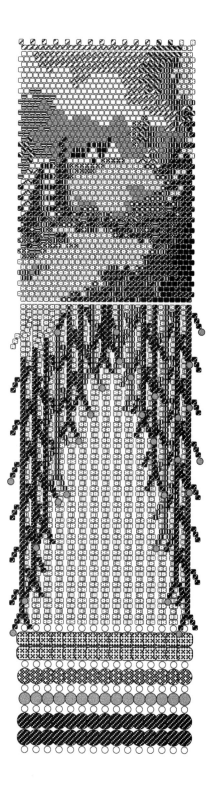

▨	DB 78	Lined Aqua Mist AB
▦	DB 80	Lined Pale Lavender AB
☐	DB 201	White Pearl
▧	DB 252	Ceylon Grey
■	DB 325	Matte Metallic Blue Iris
◪	DB 327	Matte Metallic Teal Iris
▥	DB 373	Matte Metallic Leaf Green
◨	DB 374	Matte Metallic Seafoam Green
▦	DB 742	Matte Transparent Topaz
▤	DB 855	Matte Transparent Tangerine AB
▩	DB 856	Matte Transparent Red Orange AB
▩	DB 857	Matte Transparent Light Amethyst AB
▥	DB 863	Matte Transparent Shark Grey AB
▨	DB 883	Matte Opaque Cream AB

* Base Row: 60 Beads
    31 - Front Design (Row #6)
    29 - Back done in:
        DB 883 Matte Opaque Cream AB

Total number of rows in design: 47

Purse total dimensions: 2" x 6 1/2"
     Bag: 2" x 2 1/2"
     Fringe: 4"

Field of Flowers

Attach Strap

Attach Strap

Lace ►

*

© 1998 Barbara E. Elbe

Fold | 60 55 45 35 25 20 15 13/10 13 20 25 35 45 55 60 | Fold

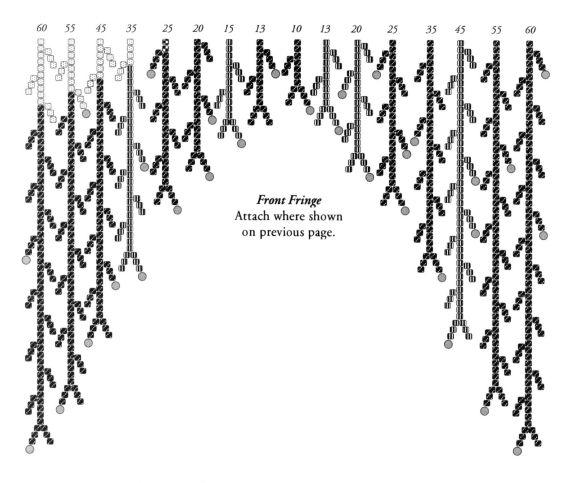

Front Fringe
Attach where shown
on previous page.

Trim Beads

○	103 --	2 mm Gold Filled Beads
●	39 --	2 mm Carnelian
●	23 --	3 mm Carnelian
●	19 --	4 mm Red Jasper
●	34 --	4 mm Unakite
▦	42 --	6 mm Matte Topaz AB

DB 883 Matte Opaque Cream AB (60 each)

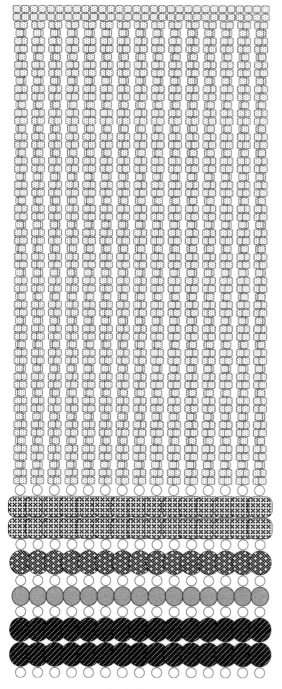

Back Fringe

Strap
Follow illustration below using a variation of the 24" Peyote Style Strap explained on page 10.

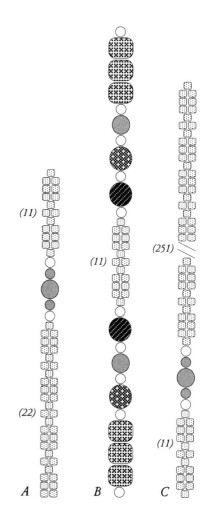

(11)

(22)

(11)

(11)

(251)

(11)

A   B   C

White Tailed Deer

▤	DB 10	Black
■	DB 25	Metallic Blue Iris
▥	DB 121	Dark Topaz Gold Luster
▦	DB 201	White Pearl
▧	DB 205	Ceylon Beige
▢	DB 221	Gild Lined White Opal
▨	DB 327	Matte Metallic Teal Green
▦	DB 374	Matte Metallic Seafoam Green
▦	DB 377	Matte Metallic Dark Grey Blue
⊠	DB 769	Matte Transparent Cocoa Brown
▤	DB 853	Matte Transparent Dark Topaz AB
▨	DB 857	Matte Transparent Light Amethyst AB
▦	DB 901	Lined Shimmering Rose Gold (Beige)

* Base Row: 60 Beads
   Front & Back of Design

Total number of rows in design: 51

Purse total dimensions: 2" x 7"
   Bag: 2" x 2 3/4"
   Fringe: 4 1/4"

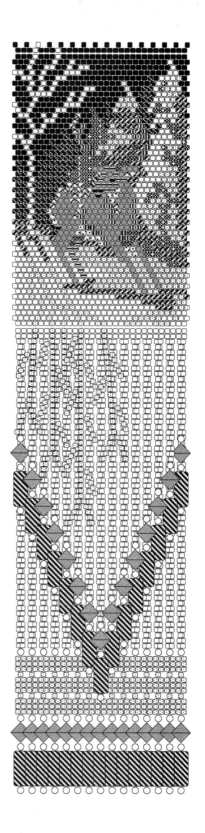

California Quail

Marsh Mallards
Shadow Pony

Ol' Saint Nicholas
Colonial Lady

Pheasant in Flight
Field of Flowers

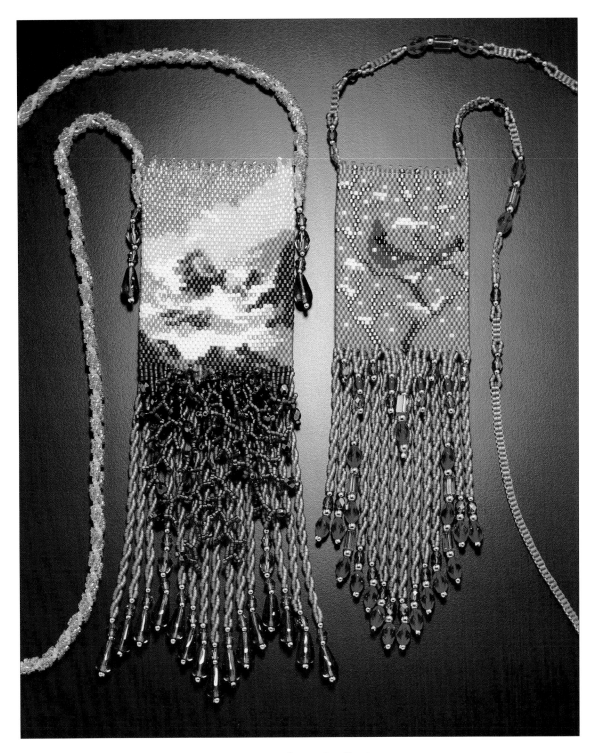

Crashing Surf
Cardinals in Winter

Peacock
White Tailed Deer

Iris Bouquet
Girl by the Sea

Cockatiel
Birch Forest

White Tailed Deer

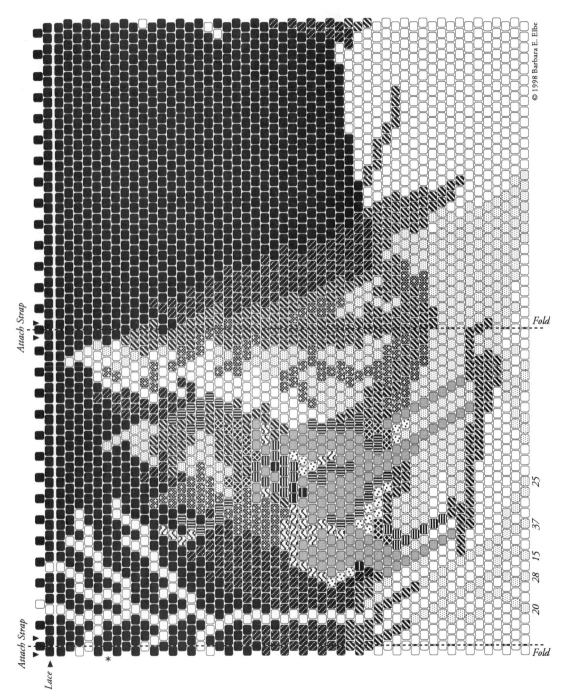

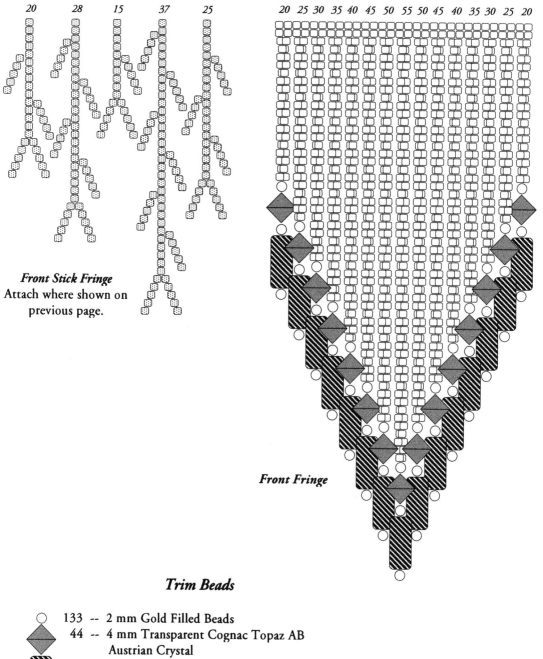

Front Stick Fringe
Attach where shown on
previous page.

Front Fringe

Trim Beads

○ 133 -- 2 mm Gold Filled Beads

◆ 44 -- 4 mm Transparent Cognac Topaz AB
Austrian Crystal

▮ 35 -- 4 x 10 mm 5-Sided Clear Amethyst

DB 221 Gild Lined White Opal (60 each)
DB 374 Matte Metallic Seafoam (11 each)

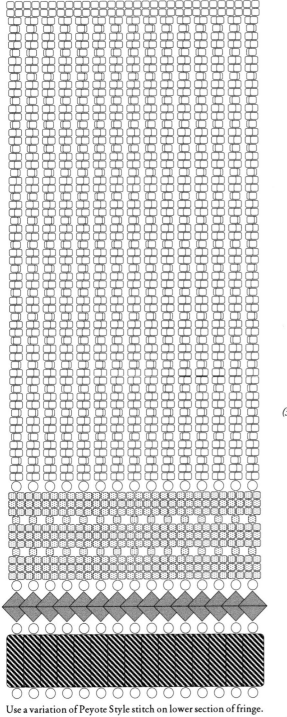

Use a variation of Peyote Style stitch on lower section of fringe.

Strap
Follow illustration below. Strap has sections done with two separate strands of beads, and sections including a variation of 24" Peyote Style Strap explained on page 10.

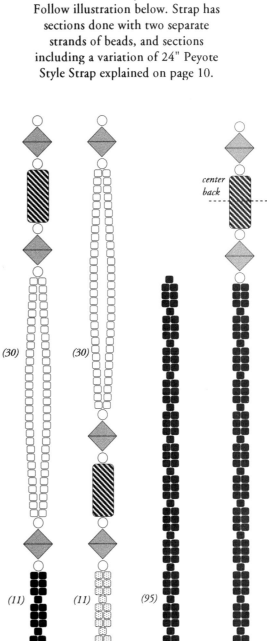

center back

(30)   (30)

(95)

(11)   (11)

A   B   C   D

35

California Quail

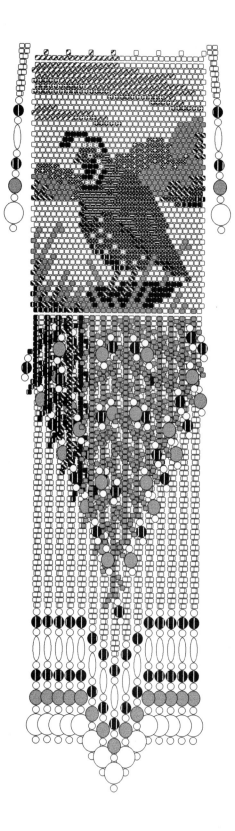

- ■ DB 25 Metallic Blue Iris
- ▦ DB 54 Lined Peach AB
- ▨ DB 80 Lined Pale Lavender AB
- ☐ DB 203 Ceylon Light Yellow
- ▨ DB 233 Lined Crystal/Yellow Luster
- ◩ DB 272 Lined Topaz/Yellow AB
- ▩ DB 307 Matte Metallic Grey
- ▦ DB 351 Matte White
- ⊡ DB 681 Semi-Matte Silver Lined Squash
- ▨ DB 742 Matte Transparent Topaz
- ❙❙ DB 773 Matte Translucent Cherrywood
- ⊗ DB 853 Matte Transparent Dark Topaz AB
- ≣ DB 863 Matte Transparent Shark Grey AB

* Base Row: 60 Beads
    31 - Front Design (Row #6)
    29 - Back done in:
        DB 203 Ceylon Light Yellow

Total number of rows in design: 47

Purse total dimensions: 2" x 6 7/8 "
    Bag: 2" x 2 5/8"
    Fringe: 4 1/4

California Quail

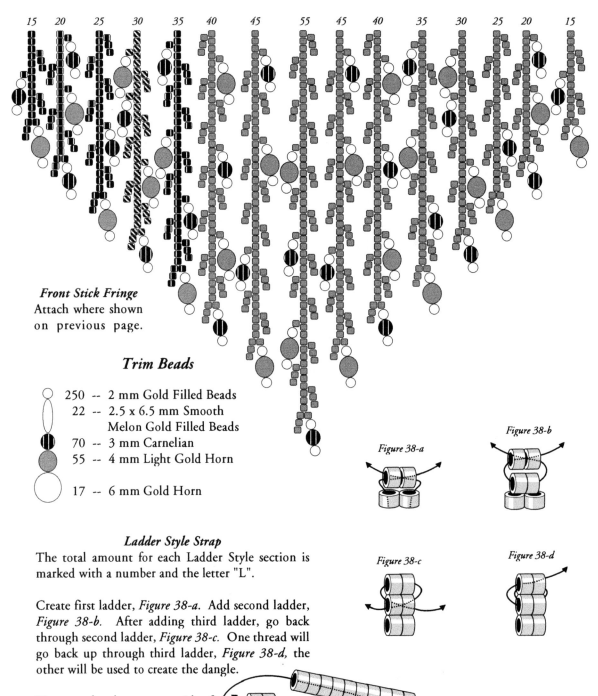

15 20 25 30 35 40 45 55 45 40 35 30 25 20 15

Front Stick Fringe
Attach where shown
on previous page.

Trim Beads

250 -- 2 mm Gold Filled Beads
22 -- 2.5 x 6.5 mm Smooth
      Melon Gold Filled Beads
70 -- 3 mm Carnelian
55 -- 4 mm Light Gold Horn

17 -- 6 mm Gold Horn

Figure 38-a

Figure 38-b

Ladder Style Strap
The total amount for each Ladder Style section is
marked with a number and the letter "L".

Figure 38-c

Figure 38-d

Create first ladder, *Figure 38-a*. Add second ladder,
Figure 38-b. After adding third ladder, go back
through second ladder, *Figure 38-c*. One thread will
go back up through third ladder, *Figure 38-d*, the
other will be used to create the dangle.

To create dangle, come out side of
second ladder (white arrow), add
dangle, twist. Run back through

Figure 38-e

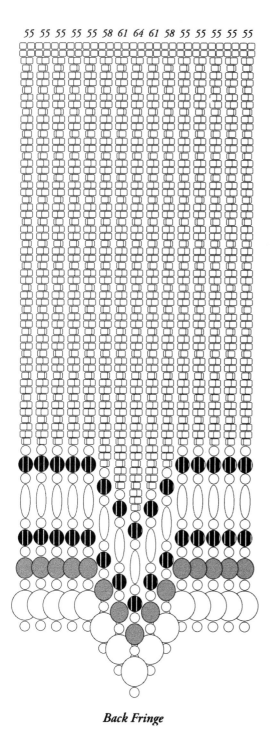

55 55 55 55 55 58 61 64 61 58 55 55 55 55 55

Back Fringe

other side of second ladder and back up through third ladder, *Figure 38-e*. Continue with rest of strap.

Repeat on other end. After creating fifth ladder, go back through fourth ladder and add dangle.

Make sure when tying off, that dangles are hanging on the outer side of strap.

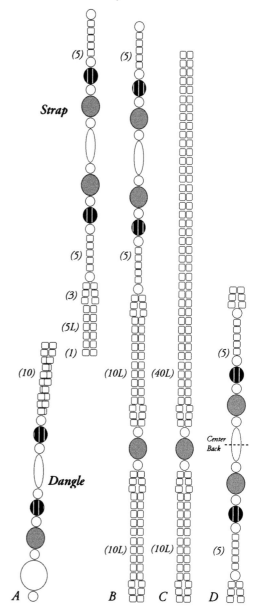

Strap

(5) *(5)*

(5) *(5)*

(3)

(5L)

(1)

(10) *(10L)* *(40L)*

(5)

Center
Back

Dangle

(10L) *(10L)*

(5)

A *B* *C* *D*

Marsh Mallards

■ DB 25 Metallic Blue Iris
▨ DB 27 Metallic Teal Iris
▨ DB 57 Lined Sky Blue AB
▨ DB 78 Lined Aqua Mist AB
▨ DB 80 Lined Pale Lavender AB
☐ DB 201 White Pearl
▨ DB 203 Ceylon Light Yellow
▨ DB 252 Ceylon Grey
▨ DB 272 Lined Topaz/Yellow
▨ DB 376 Matte Metallic Light Grey Blue
⊠ AQ 564 Galvanized Russet
▨ DB 749 Matte Transparent Grey
▨ DB 852 Matte Light Topaz AB
▥ DB 901 Lined Crystal Shim. Rose Gold (Beige)

*   Base Row: 60 Beads
        32 - Front Design (Row #6)
        28 - Back done in:
            DB 376 Matte Metallic Light Grey Blue

Total number of rows in design: 47

Purse total dimensions: 2" x 7 1/8 "
        Bag: 2" x 2 1/2"
        Fringe: 4 5/8

Marsh Mallards

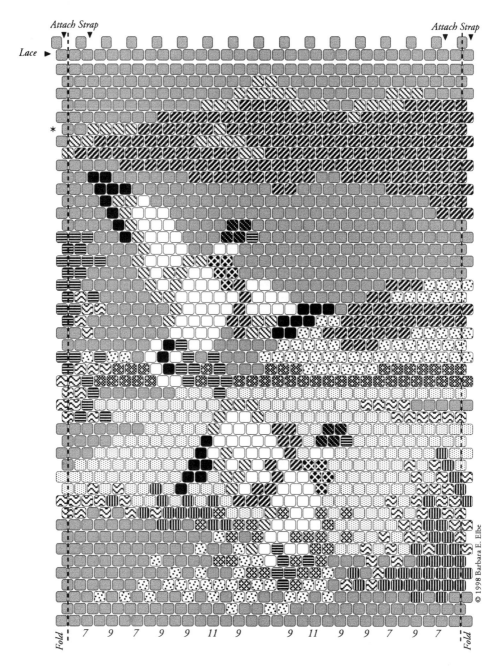

Trim Beads

○	78 -- 2 mm Gold Filled Beads
●	66 -- 3 mm Gold Filled Beads
○	4 -- 4 mm Mother of Pearl
○	29 -- 6 mm Mother of Pearl
◉	24 -- 4 mm Light Topaz Fire Polish Crystal
▦	45 -- TD1830 - Size 8/o Lined Aqua/Teal Luster Triangle Beads
▢	22 -- 4 x 6 mm Clear Light Blue AB 5-Sided Beads
▤	22 -- 4 x 6 mm Clear Topaz AB 5-Sided Beads

Front Fringe

The front fringe is done using DB 376 along with trim as shown. The number along the top of illustration above and along bottom of previous page indicate the number of DB beads used, and where they are positioned.

• Both front and back fringe on pattern take approximately 4 yards of thread.

1. Working left to right, come out of purse at first number (7) pick up DB beads add trim beads, go back through trim beads, add DB. Go up (7) bead over.

2. Down (9) to left, add beads and up second (9) bead to right. Make sure this loop is in front of previous loop.

3. Down (9) to left and up second (9) to right. Also in front of the last loop.

4. Down (11) to left add beads, up (11) to right. This is center loop and is last front loop.

5. Now go down (9) to left, up second (9) to right this time placing loop behind center loop.

6. Down (9) to left, add beads and go up (9) to right. This loop is also behind last.

7. Down (7) to left and up (7) to right and behind..

8. Turn to back and complete back fringe.

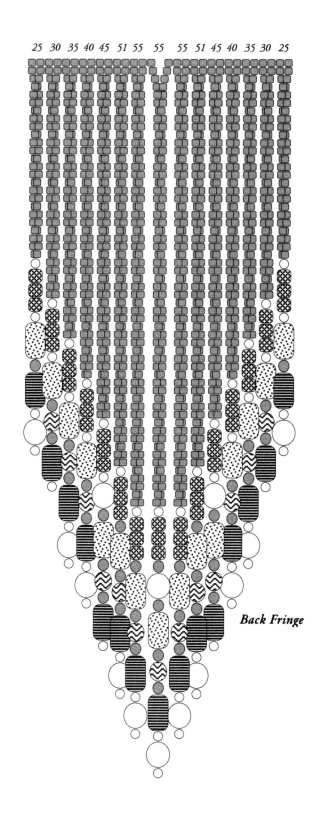

25 30 35 40 45 51 55   55 51 45 40 35 30 25

Back Fringe

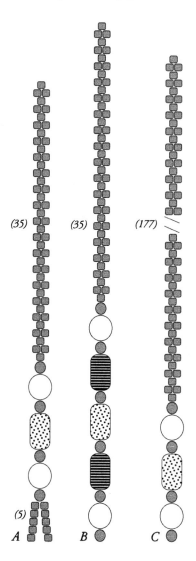

Strap
Follow illustration below
using 24" Peyote Style Strap
explained on page 10.

(35)   *(35)*   *(177)* //

(5)

A   B   C

Pheasant In Flight

- ■ DB 25 Metallic Blue Iris
- ◧ DB 29 Metallic Medium Bronze Iris
- ▨ DB 78 Lined Aqua Mist AB
- ▤ DB 80 Lined Pale Lavender AB
- ▥ DB 121 Dark Topaz Gold Luster
- ▨ DB 161 Opaque Orange AB
- ☐ DB 201 White Pearl
- ▨ DB 203 Ceylon Light Yellow
- ▨ DB 205 Ceylon Beige
- ▨ DB 272 Lined Topaz/Yellow AB
- ▨ DB 745 Matte Transparent Light Red
- ▨ DB 749 Matte Transparent Grey
- ▨ DB 769 Matte Transparent Cocoa Brown
- ▨ DB 771 Matte Translucent Sand
- ▨ DB 791 Dyed Matte Opaque Red Red
- ▬ DB 853 Matte Transparent Dark Topaz AB
- ▨ DB 857 Matte Transparent Light Amethyst AB
- ▨ DB 901 Lined Crystal Shim. Rose Gold (Beige)

* Base Row: 60 Beads

    31 - Front Design (Row #6)

    29 - Back done in:

        DB 203 Ceylon Light Yellow

Total number of rows in design: 47

    Purse total dimensions: 2" x 6 5/8"

        Bag: 2" x 2 5/8"

        Fringe: 4"

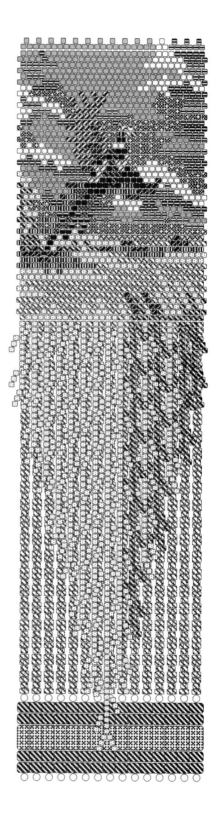

Pheasant In Flight

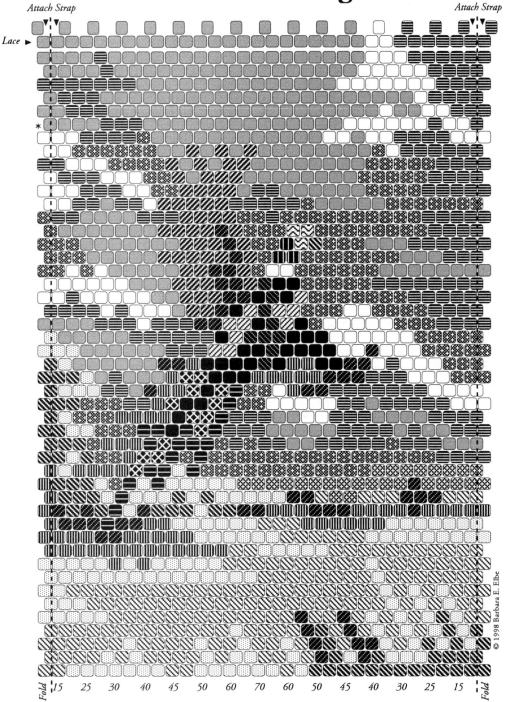

Attach Strap

Attach Strap

Lace ▶

Fold   15   25   30   40   45   50   60   70   60   50   45   40   30   25   15   Fold

45

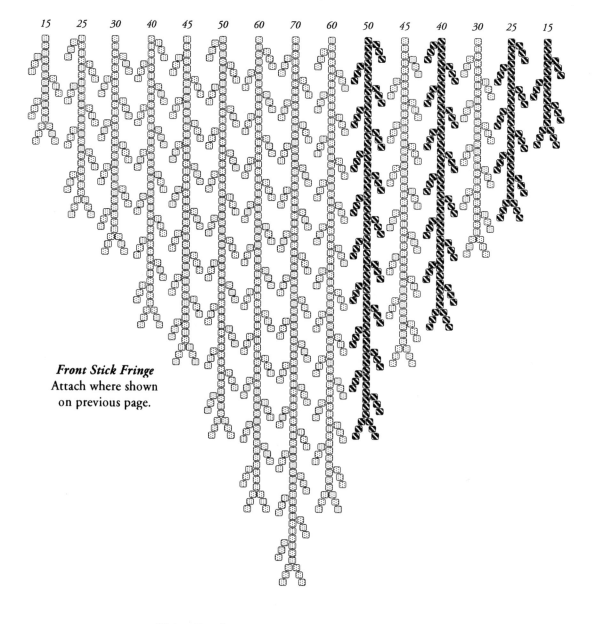

15 25 30 40 45 50 60 70 60 50 45 40 30 25 15

Front Stick Fringe
Attach where shown
on previous page.

Trim Beads

○ 42 -- 2 mm Gold Filled Beads

⬚ 23 -- 4 x 6 mm Light Blue AB 5-Sided Beads

◣ 84 -- TC 1166 - Size 5/o - Lined Gold Mauve AB
     Triangle Beads

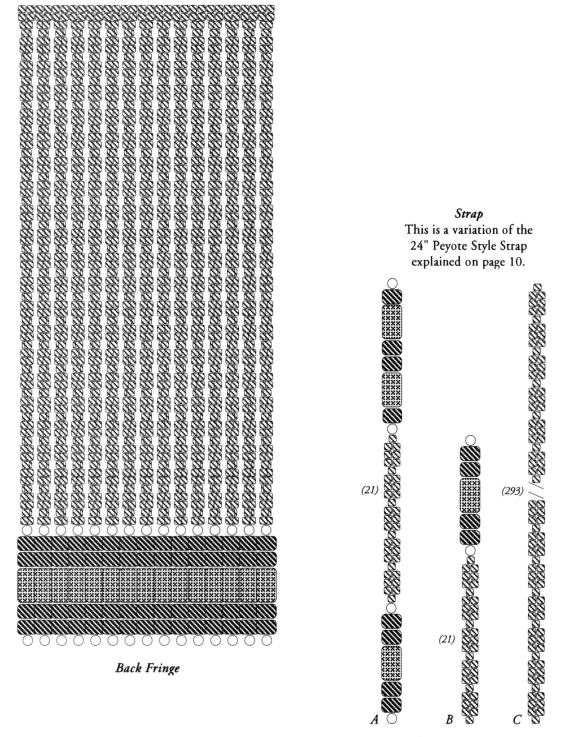

DB 203 Ceylon Light Yellow (60 each)

Back Fringe

Strap
This is a variation of the
24" Peyote Style Strap
explained on page 10.

(21)

(293)

(21)

A

B

C

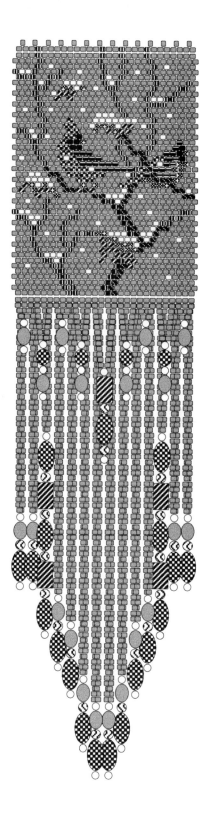

Cardinals In Winter

	DB	10	Black
	DB	54	Lined Peach AB
	DB	105	Gold Luster Trans. Dark Red
	DB	121	Dark Topaz Gold Luster
	DB	201	White Pearl
	DB	272	Lined Topaz/Yellow AB
	DB	307	Matte Metallic Grey
	DB	325	Matte Metallic Blue Iris
	DB	697	Semi-Matte Silver Lined Grey
	DB	774	Dyed Matte Transparent Red
	DB	857	Matte Transp. Light Amethyst AB

* Base Row: 56 Beads
      29 - Front Design (Row #6)
      27 - Back done in:
            DB 857 Matte Transparent Light
                  Amethyst AB

Total number of rows in design: 45

      Purse total dimensions: 1 7/8" x 6 1/2 "
            Bag: 1 7/8" x 2 1/2"
            Fringe: 4

Cardinals in Winter

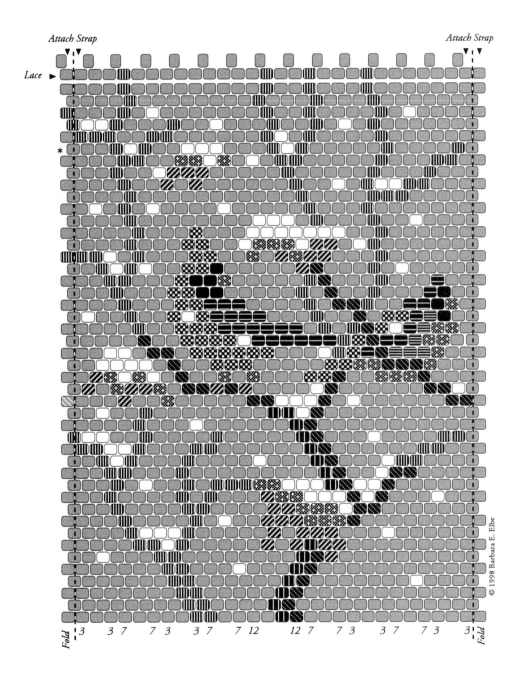

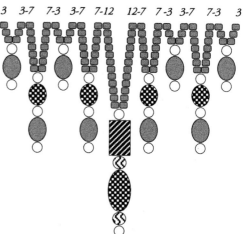

Front Fringe

1. Working left to right, add three DB 857 at upper left corner. Add trim beads, go back up through trim, add three DB beads and up second number to right (3).

2. Down third number (7) with seven DB beads, up next (7) over.

3. Continue along the bottom of purse matching numbers as on previous page.

Trim Beads

76 -- 2 mm Gold Filled Beads

28 -- 3 mm Gold Filled Beads

30 -- 4 mm Dark Amethyst AB Fire Polish Crystal

4 -- 4 mm Clear Red Druk

25 -- 5 x 7 mm Transp. Ruby Red Fire Polish Crystal

8 -- 4 x 6 mm Clear Topaz AB 5-Sided Glass Beads

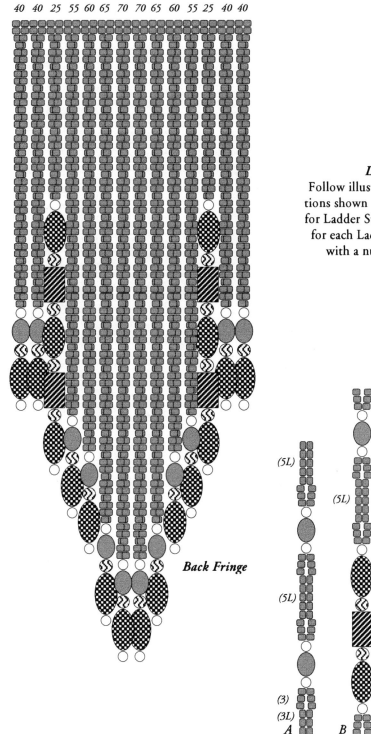

40 40 25 55 60 65 70 70 65 60 55 25 40 40

Back Fringe

Ladder Style Strap
Follow illustration below using instructions shown on Page 38, *Figures 38-a & b* for Ladder Style Strap. The total amount for each Ladder Style section is marked with a number and the letter "L".

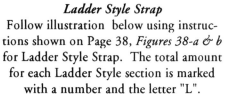

Center Back

(5L)

(5L)

(5L)

(5L)

(76L)

(5L)

(3)
(3L)

A   B   C   D   E

51

Cockatiel

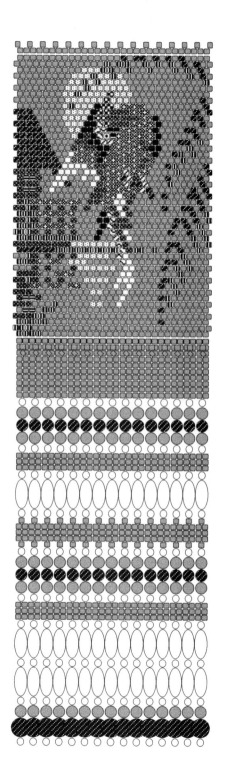

- ⊙ DB 10 Black
- ▨ DB 56 Lined Magenta AB
- ▦ DB 70 Lined Rose Pink AB
- ▨ DB 160 Opaque Yellow AB
- ☐ DB 201 White Pearl
- ▧ DB 203 Ceylon Light Yellow
- ▨ DB 233 Lined Crystal Yellow Luster
- ▨ DB 234 Pale Pink Pearl
- ▨ DB 252 Ceylon Grey
- ■ DB 307 Matte Metallic Grey
- ▤ DB 686 Semi-Matte Silver Lined Jonquil
- ▬ DB 855 Matte Transparent Tangerine AB
- ▨ DB 863 Matte Transparent Shark Grey AB
- ▥ DB 902 Lined Crystal Shimmering Rosy Pink

* Base Row: 60 Beads
      31 - Front Design (Row #6)
      29 - Back done in:
          DB 54 Lined Peach AB

Total number of rows in design: 47

     Purse total dimensions: 2" x 6 5/8 "
         Bag: 2" x 2 5/8"
         Fringe: 4"

Cockatiel

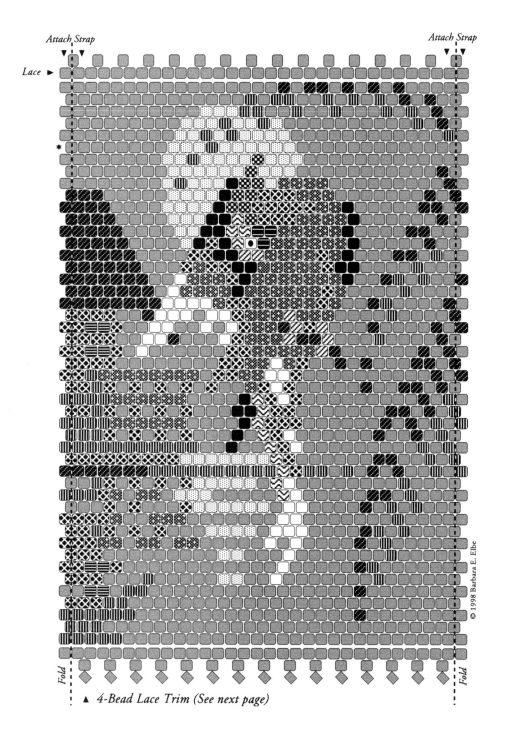

Attach Strap

Attach Strap

Lace ▶

*

© 1998 Barbara E. Elbe

Fold

Fold

▲ 4-Bead Lace Trim (See next page)

4-Bead Lace Trim

This trim gives a lacy effect and can added to the top or bottom edge of a purse.

Figure 54-a

1. Coming out one corner of purse, pick up three DB beads.

2. Go around last bead closest to needle and through second bead only. *Figure 54-a*

3. Pick up one DB bead, go through next bead over on purse. *Figure 54-b*

Figure 54-a

4. Pull everything together. Adjust.

5. Continue along edge of purse as shown.

Trim Beads

174 -- 2 mm Gold Filled Beads
53 -- 4 x 7 mm Antique Bone

91 -- 4 mm Satin Rose Druk
34 -- 4 mm Violet Fossil
19 -- 6 mm Violet Fossil

DB 70 Lined Rose Pink AB

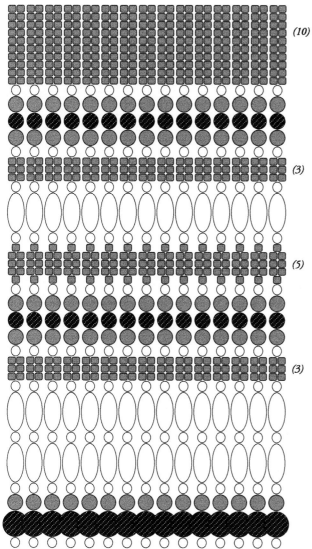

(10)

(3)

(5)

(3)

Back Fringe

Strap
Follow Illustration below using a
variation of 24" Peyote Style Strap
explained on Page 10.

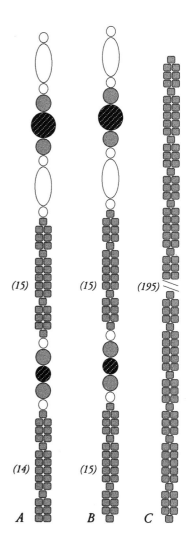

(15) *(15)* *(195)*

(14) *(15)*

A   B   C

55

Vertical Brick Stitch
Instructions

Vertical Brick Stitch is brick stitch worked flat following a pattern vertically instead of horizontally. The sides are sewed together instead of the bottom. Use the same basic instructions as horizontal brick stitch for starting the base row. *Pages 13 & 14*

1. Cut a section of size D Nymo® thread 5 yards long, wax.

2. Place needle just 2-3 inches in from one end.

3. Pick up two beads and place 2 1/2 yards in (halfway point on thread). This will allow 2 1/2 yards of thread to start the left half of the design and another 2 1/2 yards for the beginning of the right half of the design.

4. Create the base row (usually the center row) with the number of beads stated in the pattern . DO NOT JOIN ENDS TOGETHER. Turn.

5. **Second Row** Without increasing or decreasing on the end of the row the beads will naturally taper to a point. To start the beginning of a regular row, (using hidden outer thread technique) pick up two beads the same way you would to increase a row by one bead. Instead of attaching to the first loop of work, attach to the second. *Figure 56-a*

Now loop back through the first bead added (white arrow), back up through the second and pull them close together. *Figure 56-b* Continue with the rest of the row.

6. Increase or decrease as pattern shows giving a sculptured effect along top and side edges. Vertical Brick Stitch is done flat, bent in half when completed and joined by stitching up the sides. *Figure 56-c*

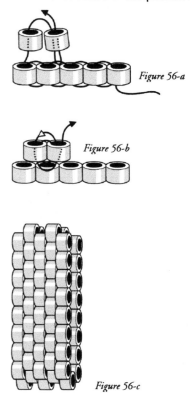

Figure 56-a

Figure 56-b

Figure 56-c

Knowing how to increase and decrease allows you to be as creative as you wish. This is how sculpturing is achieved. Some of the techniques shown here may not be used in the following patterns but can be helpful in further projects.

Increasing at Beginning To increase by just one extra bead, pick up two beads instead of the usual one, attach to the same place as you would have the one. *Figure 57-a*

Figures 57-a   Figures 57-b

To increase the row by two beads at one end. Start at the white arrow, *Figure 57-b*, go back through the first bead on the row, pick up a new bead, loop around and follow the arrows back to where you started. A row can be increased by as many beads as you wish in this fashion. Just keep adding to the end before going back to where you started.

Increasing at End This can be done in a couple of ways. One is to pick up a new bead, go down through bead on the previous row, then back through the new bead. *Figure 57-c* If there is an end thread on the previous row (end threads are not on every row), the new bead can be attached there. *Figure 57-d*

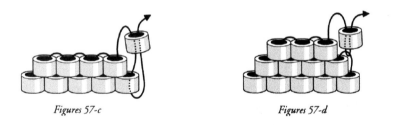

Figures 57-c   Figures 57-d

To increase a row on end by two or more beads, follow directions above. *Figure 57-c or 57-d* Add as shown starting at white arrow. *Figure 57-e*

Figure 57-e

The direction the needle ends up pointing after increasing can be very important to the continuation of the design. *Figure 58-a* shows how to change that direction. Begin at the white arrow.

Figure 58-a

Figure 58-a is the same as *Figure 58-b* except this row is increased by three beads. On a normal increase, the needle would be facing up.

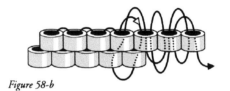

Figure 58-b

Decreasing at Beginning of Next Row Drop down to the row below and come up where the next row begins. *Figure 58-c*. Depending on how many previous rows you go down through changes how far over you will come out.

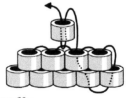

Figure 58-c

Ol' Saint Nicholas

- ● DB 10 Black
- ■ DB 25 Metallic Blue Iris
- ▨ DB 31 Bright Gold 22k
- ▨ DB 67 Lined Flesh AB
- ▥ DB 105 Gold Luster Transparent Dark Red
- ☐ DB 221 Gilt Lined White Opal
- ▨ DB 252 Ceylon Grey
- ▤ DB 325 Matte Metallic Blue Iris
- ⊠ DB 327 Matte Metallic Teal Iris
- ▨ DB 769 Matte Transparent Cocoa Brown
- ▨ DB 774 Dyed Matte Transparent Red
- ◩ DB 853 Matte Transparent Dark Topaz AB

* Base Row: 109 Beads

Total number of rows wide: 35
Total rows tall: 55

Purse total dimensions: 2 1/4" x 5 1/4 "
      Bag: 1 7/8" x 3 3/4"
      Fringe: 1 1/2"

24" Spiral Rope Strap

Using 12 yards of **Black** size D Nymo thread, follow instructions on *Page 11* for Spiral Rope Strap. Make strap 32" in length without dangle.

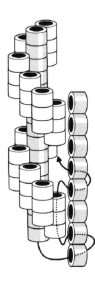

1. Starting at back left side of purse and coming out core bead, attach to purse by going through last bead on lower left corner and coming out bead above.

2. Go through 3 outer spiral beads, then back into purse as shown.

3. Follow illustration attaching to outer spiral beads that line up with edge of purse.

4. Repeat along front edge of purse.

5. Weave tail of thread into purse and cut.

Trim Beads

○   2 -- 2 mm Gold Filled Beads
●   6 -- 3 mm Gold Filled Beads
◯   2 -- 8 mm Clear AB Austrian Crystal

     4 -- 6 x 11 Topaz Teardrop

Ol' Saint Nicholas

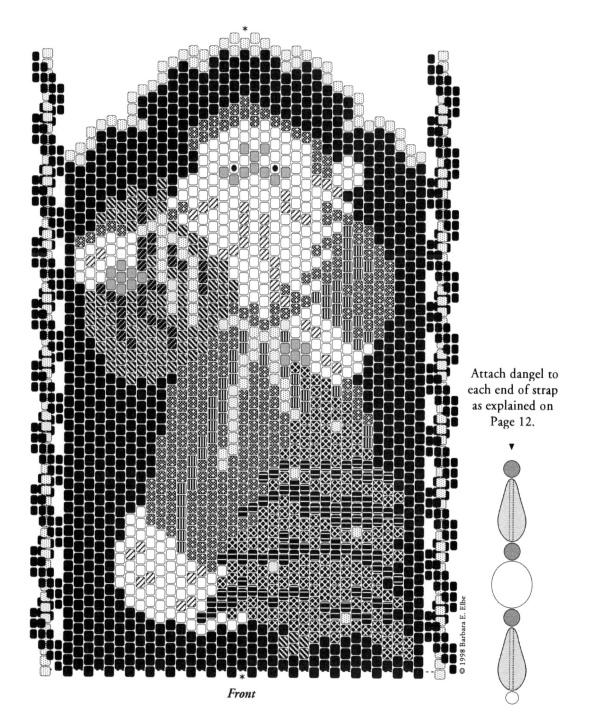

Attach dangel to
each end of strap
as explained on
Page 12.

Front

*

Begin attaching
strap to lower
back left corner
of purse ▶ - - -

Fold

© 1998 Barbara E. Elbe

*

Back

61

Merlin

- ⬤ DB 10 Black
- ☰ DB 31 Bright Gold 22k
- ▦ DB 67 Lined Flesh AB
- ▨ DB 70 Lined Rose Pink AB
- ▩ DB 108 Gold Luster Amethyst
- ⬜ DB 221 Gild Lined White Opal
- ▦ DB 325 Matte Metallic Blue Iris
- ▨ DB 686 Semi-Matte Silver Lined Jonquil
- ⬛ AQ 704 Matte Blue Purple
- ▨ DB 856 Matte Transparent Red Orange AB
- ▥ DB 905 Lined Crystal Shimmering Sky Blue

* Base Row: 87 Beads

Total number of rows wide: 35
Total rows tall: 44

Purse total dimensions: 1 7/8" x 5 3/4 "
    Bag: 2 1/8" x 3 1/8"
    Fringe: 2 5/8"

Peyote Strap

1. This stitch will take approximately 7 inches of thread per inch of strap. With that in mind, attach a 5 1/2 yard section of thread to upper left corner of hat where shown.

2. Pick up one bead (AQ 704), go through top edge of purse, pull bead into place. *Figure 62-a*

3. Pick up another bead, go through next end bead sticking out, pull into place. Turn

4. Repeat steps #2 and #3. *Figure 62-b* Add stars along side edges as shown. *Figure 62-c*

5. Continue until 24" strap is complete. Attach to other side of purse where shown. Weave in end.

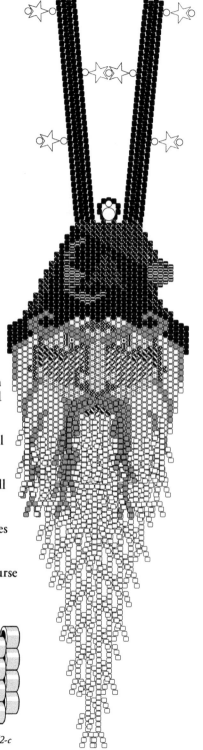

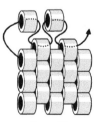

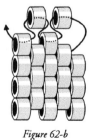

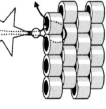

Figure 62-a

Figure 62-b

Figure 62-c

Merlin

Start at * Base Row
(beginning under the loop,
starting with AQ 704).
Loop and Mother of Pearl
bead is added later.

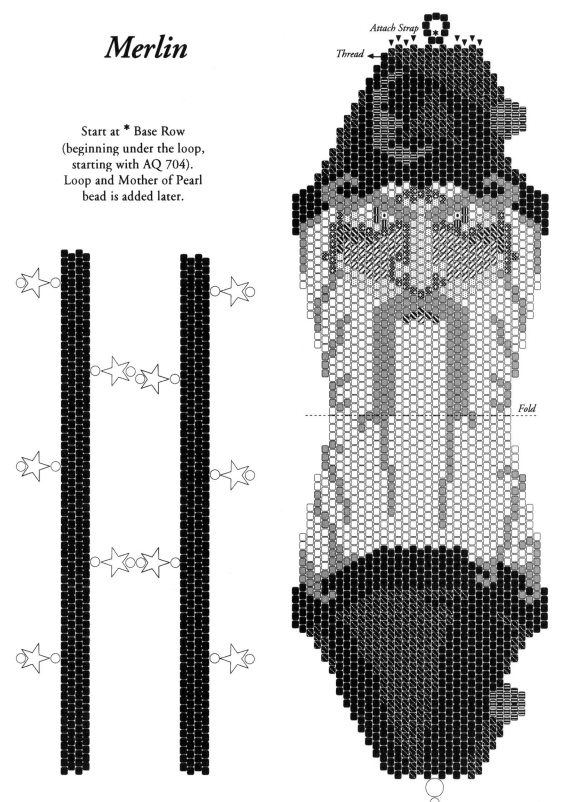

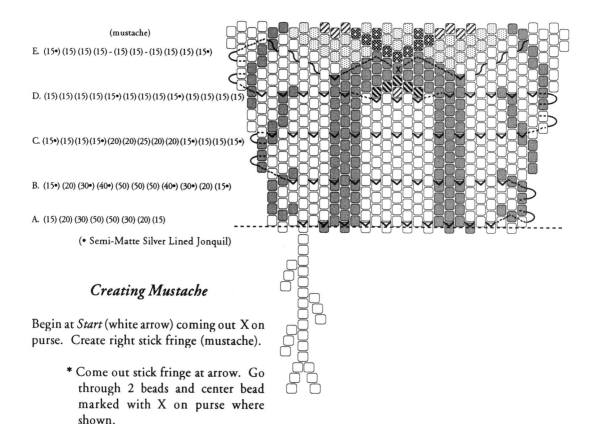

(mustache)

E. (15•) (15) (15) (15) - (15) (15) - (15) (15) (15) (15•)

D. (15) (15) (15) (15) (15•) (15) (15) (15) (15•) (15) (15) (15)

C. (15•) (15) (15) (15•) (20) (20) (25) (20) (20) (15•) (15) (15) (15•)

B. (15•) (20) (30•) (40•) (50) (50) (50) (40•) (30•) (20) (15•)

A. (15) (20) (30) (50) (50) (30) (20) (15)

(• Semi-Matte Silver Lined Jonquil)

Creating Mustache

Begin at *Start* (white arrow) coming out X on purse. Create right stick fringe (mustache).

> * Come out stick fringe at arrow. Go through 2 beads and center bead marked with X on purse where shown.

Repeat on left side ending up at X shown on pattern. Continue with rest of beard on right side of face, as shown on pattern.

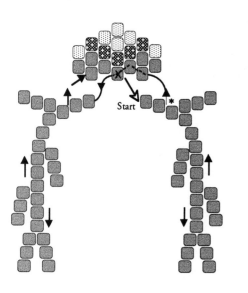

Trim Beads

10 -- 6 mm Howlite Stars
21 -- 2 mm Gold Filled Beads
1 -- 4 mm Mother of Pearl

Square Stitch

When completed, square stitch looks very much like loom weave. Unlike brick stitch or peyote stitch, which has the beads arranged in a pattern resembling stacked bricks and only has one vertical or horizontal line in the work, square stitch has the beads directly above, below and side by side allowing for both vertical and horizontal straight lines in the work. Best of all, when the beading is completed, there is only the single beading thread left to work into the piece instead of all the loose threads associated with loom work.

I usually start my pieces at the back right hand corner. I know it is boring doing only one color when first starting out on a new project, but it has to be completed sometime and this gives good practice with the weave. Think how exciting it will be when you finally get to the front. Keep an even tension making sure the piece keeps even top and bottom edges.

The beads in square stitch have a slight tilt to them caused by the way the thread loops around in weaving the piece together. Just think of this as a nap. All work should be done in ONE direction (left to right or right to left). If worked in two different directions, the beads will tilt two different ways.

Unlike brick and peyote stitch, the thread between the beads will show in square stitch. This makes choosing the thread color of thread a little more difficult. Dark color threads tend to dull light colored and transparent beads giving them a greyish look. The patterns in this book have all been done with white size D Nymo (except where noted). The thread showing gives somewhat of a antique look.

Start with a section of thread approximately two yards in length. Add a single bead about 10 inched from the end as a stop bead. This bead is mainly to keep the other beads from sliding off the end, it doesn't matter if it doesn't hold in place very well, just slide it back in place occasionally. The bead will be removed later and the end of the thread will be worked in into the piece.

String the amount of beads listed for the base row.

To start next row, pick up a bead and go up last bead strung, down through the bead added. Pull beads together. This bead will be the first bead of the next row. All beads are connected side by side. *Figure 65-a*

Pick up another bead, go up second to the last bead strung, down through the bead added and pull beads together. *Figure 65-b*

Repeat until all originally strung beads have a bead next to them, turn.

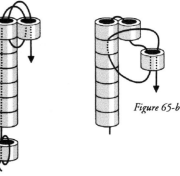

Figure 65-b

Figure 65-a

Increasing

To increase a row on one end of a design, add the amount of beads needed for the increase plus one. In the example to the left, the row is being increased by two beads; therefore, you would need to add three beads. The extra bead will be the first bead of the next row. Attach the bead in the same fashion as explained earlier and also shown in *Figure 66-a*.

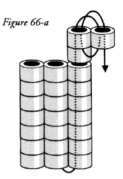

Figure 66-a

Pick up a second bead and attach as shown. Continue to the end of the row. *Figure 66-b*

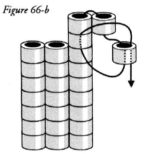

Figure 66-b

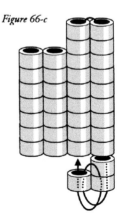

Figure 66-c

To increase a row of beads on the other end, add amount of beads needed for increase plus one (as done before). Increase the row at this end before going on to the rest of the design. *Figure 66-c*

Continue adding beads as shown, (starting at white arrow) until the space between the increase is filled.

When the last bead is in place, go through the last bead of the original piece of work and out the beads of the increased row. This secures the increased section to the main part of the design. *Figure 67-a*

Now you are ready to start the next row.

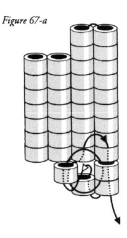

Figure 67-a

Decreasing

To decrease on the next row, go down through the previous row (white arrow) and exit the bead on the last row completed where you wish to start the new row. *Figure 67-b*

To decrease on the end of a row, stop at desired length. Continue with next row. *Figure 67-c*

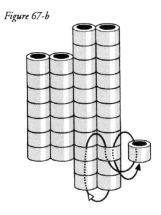

Figure 67-b

Adding Thread and Tying Off

There is no need to knot. Weave in the end, zig zagging through the rows. It is best to do this on the backside of work. Since so much thread has already been woven through the piece, the last bit of thread may show more than you wish.

Connecting Front to Back

To connect front and back together down the side, use the same stitch using the beads already there.

Go down through the first bead on the back, up through the first bead on the front, down two beads in the back and pull together. Repeat to the bottom and weave in the end of the thread as described above. Stitch bottom of purse together.

Figure 67-c

Lady Guinevere

- ◼ DB 10 Black
- ▤ DB 54 Lined Peach AB
- ▨ DB 56 Lined Magenta AB
- ▨ DB 67 Lined Flesh AB
- ▨ DB 70 Lined Rose Pink AB
- ▢ DB 201 White Pearl
- ▨ DB 203 Ceylon Light Yellow
- ▨ DB 233 Lined Crystal/Yellow Luster
- ▨ DB 307 Matte Metallic Grey
- ▥ DB 769 Matte Transparent Cocoa Brown
- ▥ DB 774 Dyed Matte Transparent Red
- ▨ DB 856 Matte Transparent Red Orange AB
- ▨ DB 905 Lined Crystal Shimmering Sky Blue

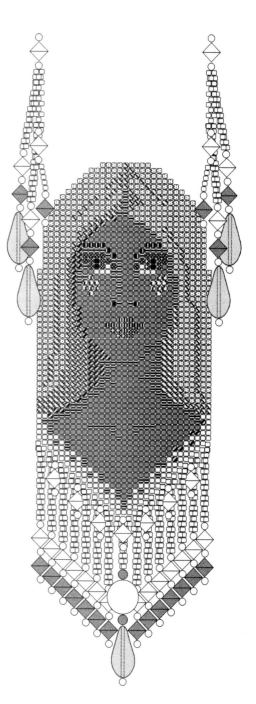

* Base Row: 32 Beads

On this purse, start at front, lower left corner
marked with *****. String the first row on left front
side of purse.

- This starts the purse with two rows of the
  same length, and lines up the pattern for
  the extended parts of the purse.

Working right to left, add the first row of the back
(same length as front row). Work across the back,
then around to the front. Join to the single front
row.

Total number of rows across: 31
Total rows down: 66

    Purse total dimensions: 2 1/8" x 5 1/2 "
       Bag: 2 1/8" x 4"
       Fringe: 1 1/2"

Lady Guinevere

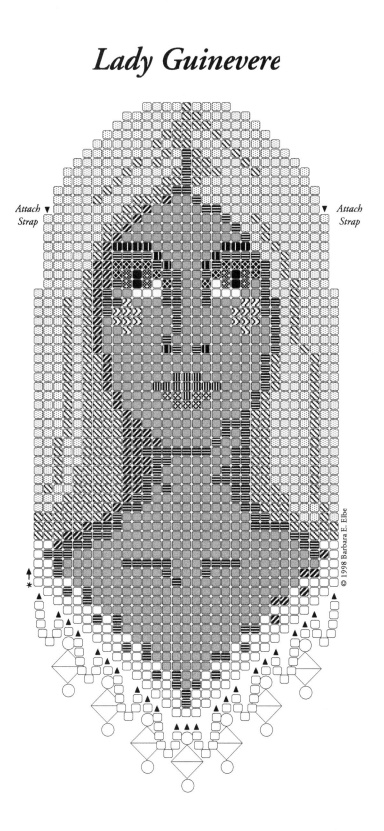

Attach ▼
Strap

▼ *Attach*
Strap

© 1998 Barbara E. Elbe

Use two 40 inch sections of waxed thread. Attach to purse where shown. Add necessary beads and crystals up to small lower arrow, page 71. Add first two DB beads of Peyote Style Strap, shown below. With one of the two threads (starting at white arrow), go down DB on the left, add dangle, twist and back up DB on right. *Figure 70-a* Make sure that dangle is hanging facing out. Alternate thread used for dangle to keep the two threads closer to same length. Add the Peyote Style section, repeat dangle. Continue with strap.

On other end, coming out DB bead with one of the two threads, create dangle first, twist, go down DB to left, and up DB on right. *Figure 70-b* Repeat with second dangle. Make sure that all dangles are hanging facing out before tying off.

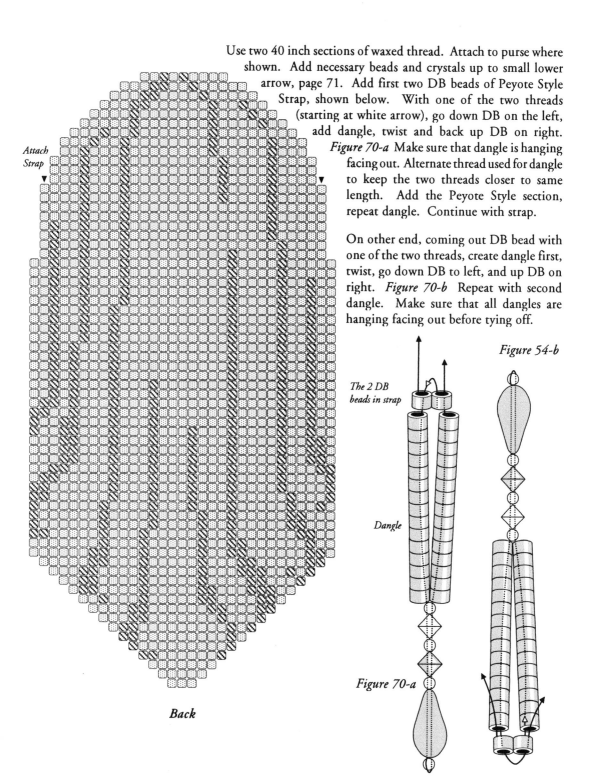

Attach Strap

Back

The 2 DB beads in strap

Figure 54-b

Dangle

Figure 70-a

Each fringe 15 DB 201 White Pearl -- Center fringe 10

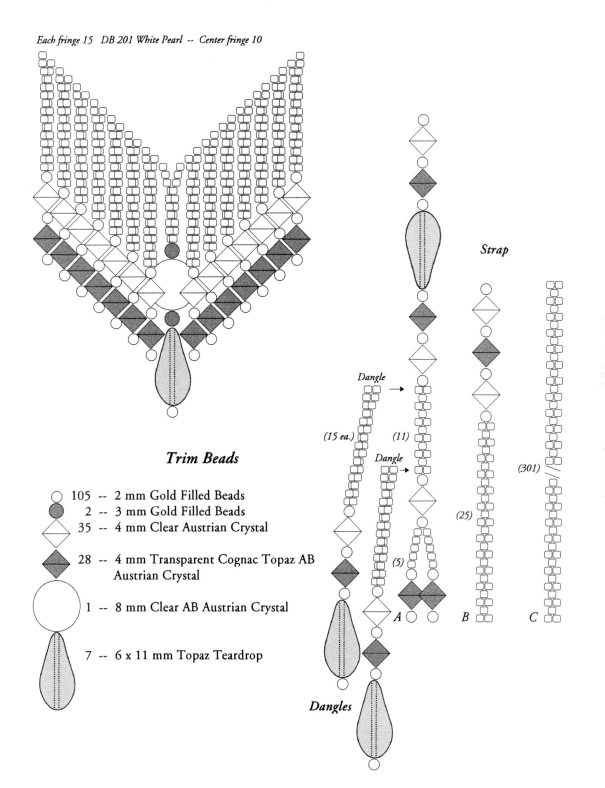

Strap

Dangle →

(15 ea.)

(11)

Dangle →

Trim Beads

(301)

○ 105 -- 2 mm Gold Filled Beads

● 2 -- 3 mm Gold Filled Beads

◇ 35 -- 4 mm Clear Austrian Crystal

◆ 28 -- 4 mm Transparent Cognac Topaz AB
Austrian Crystal

○ 1 -- 8 mm Clear AB Austrian Crystal

7 -- 6 x 11 mm Topaz Teardrop

(25)

(5)

A

B

C

Dangles

71

Colonial Lady

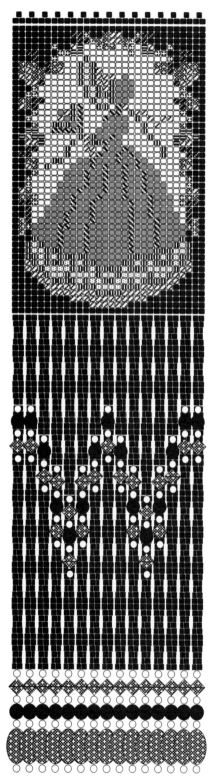

⊞	DB 46	Silver Lined Light Green
⊡	DB 70	Lined Rose Pink
■	DB 310	Matte Black
◧	DB 325	Matte Metallic Blue Iris
▥	DB 362	Matte Metallic Red AB
▦	DB 683	Semi-Matte Silver Lined Dark Ruby
▨	DB 690	Semi-Matte Silver Lined Dark Grey-Green
▨	DB 693	Semi-Matte Silver Lined Medium Blue
▤	DB 694	Semi-Matte Silver Lined Purple
☐	AQ 763	Matte Soft Peach
▨	DB 792	Dyed Matte Opaque Blue Grey
▨	DB 856	Matte Transparent Red/Orange AB

* Base Row (not shown): 47 Beads
Start at the back, lower right hand corner.

30 - Front Design Width
30 - Back done in:
    DB 310 Matte Black

Total number of rows across: 30
Total rows down: 48

• Fringe and strap done with **Black** size D
Nymo thread. Purse is done with White
size D Nymo. Black thread would cause
many of the transparent or lighter colors in
the purse to have a greyish cast.

Purse total dimensions: 2" x 6 3/4 "
    Bag: 2" x 3"
    Fringe: 3 3/4"

Colonial Lady

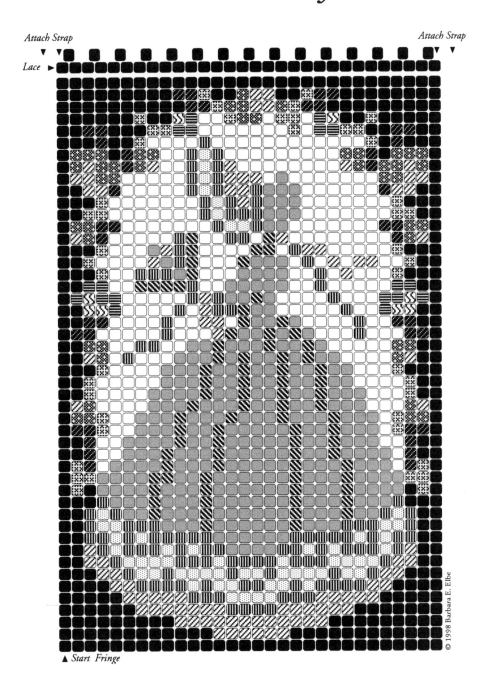

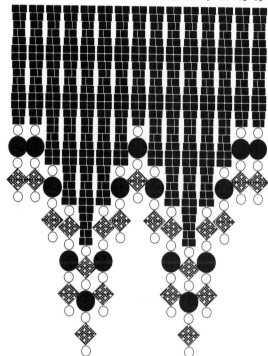

Front Fringe

15 15 20 25 30 25 20 15 20 25 30 25 20 15 15

Trim Beads

○   167 -- 2 mm Gold Filled Beads

◆   47 -- 4 mm Transparent Light Red Austrian Crystal

●   42 -- 4 mm Jet Black Fire Polish Crystal

     23 -- 5 x 7 mm Transparent Ruby Fire Polish Crystal

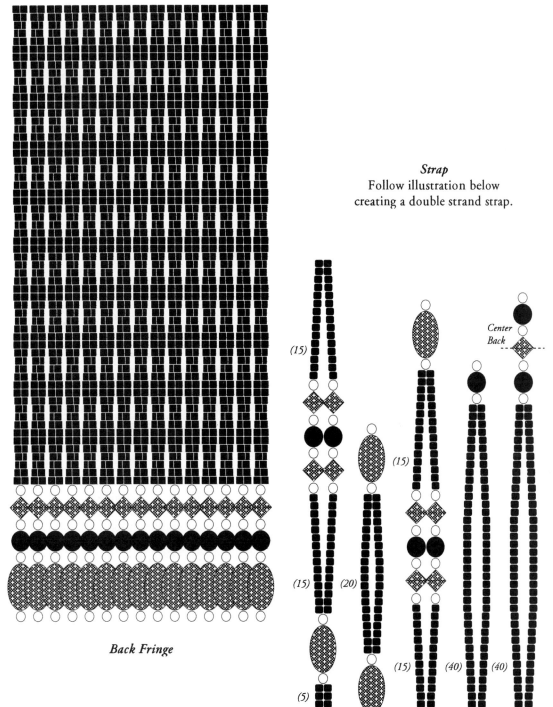

DB 310 Matte Black (60 each)

Back Fringe

Strap
Follow illustration below
creating a double strand strap.

*Center
Back*

(15)

(15)

(15)

(20)

(15)

(15)

(40)

(40)

(5)

A   B   C   D   E

Birch Forest

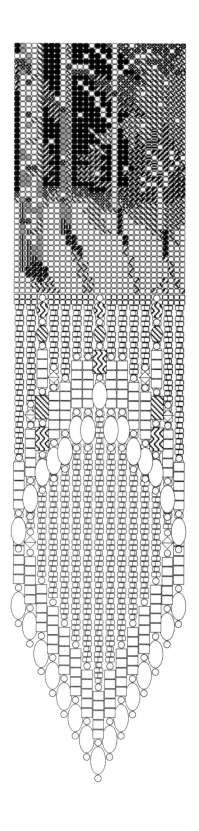

⊠	DB 10	Black
▨	DB 57	Lined Sky Blue AB
▨	DB 70	Lined Rose Pink AB
▢	DB 221	Gilt Lined White Opal
⊪	DB 307	Matte Metallic Grey
■	DB 325	Matte Metallic Blue Iris
▨	DB 327	Matte Metallic Teal Iris
▤	DB 373	Matte Metallic Leaf Green
▩	DB 856	Matte Transparent Red Orange AB
▦	DB 863	Matte Transparent Shark Grey AB
▨	DB 905	Lined Crystal Shimmering Sky Blue AB

* Base Row (not shown): 47 Beads
Start at the back, lower right hand corner.

    30 - Front Design Width
    30 - Back done in:
        DB 70 Lined Rose Pink AB

Total number of rows Across: 30
Total rows down: 47

    Purse total dimensions: 2" x 7 1/4 "
        Bag: 2" x 2 3/4"
        Fringe: 4 1/2

Birch Forest

Attach Strap ▼ ▼   Attach Strap ▼ ▼

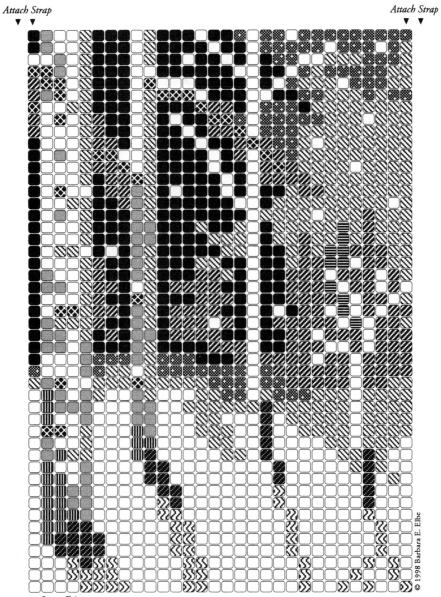

▲ Start Fringe

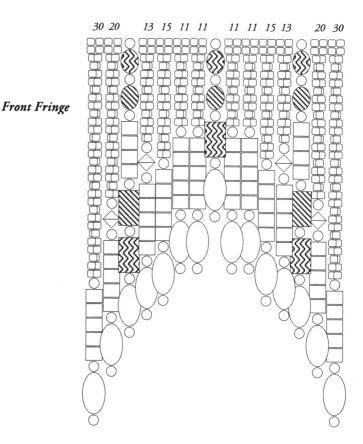

Front Fringe

30 20		13	15	11	11		11	11 15 13		20 30

143 -- TD1151 - Size 8/o Crystal AB Triangle Beads

142 -- 2 mm Sterling Silver Beads

40 -- 5 x 7 mm Clear AB Fire Polish Crystal

6 -- 4 mm Clear AB Austrian Crystal

3 -- 4 mm Light Blue AB Fire Polish Crystal

11 -- 4 x 6 mm Light Blue AB 5-Sided Glass Beads

3 -- 4 mm Light Pink AB Fire Polish Crystal

10 -- 4 x 6 mm Light Pink AB 5-Sided Glass Beads

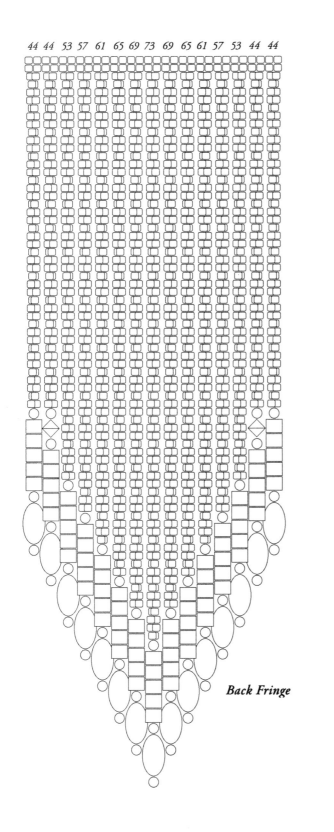

44 44 53 57 61 65 69 73 69 65 61 57 53 44 44

Back Fringe

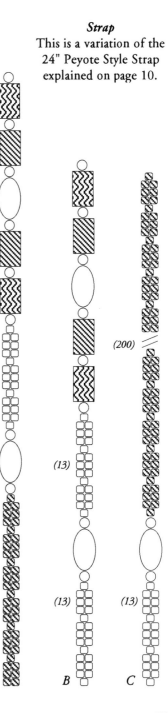

Strap
This is a variation of the
24" Peyote Style Strap
explained on page 10.

(13)

(24)

(13)

(13)

(200)

(13)

(13)

A

B

C

Shadow Pony

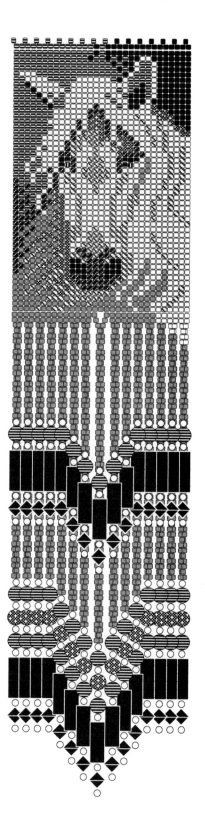

■ DB 10 Black
▧ DB 80 Lined Pale Lavender AB
☐ DB 201 White Pearl
▨ DB 252 Ceylon Grey
▤ DB 272 Lined Topaz/Yellow AB
▨ DB 307 Matte Metallic Grey
▤ DB 377 Matte Metallic Dark Grey Blue
Ⅲ DB 681 Semi-Matte Silver Lined Squash
▨ DB 863 Matte Transparent Shark Grey AB

* Base Row (not shown): 49 Beads
    31 - Front Design Width
    31 - Back done in:
        DB 10 Black

Total number of rows across: 31
Total rows down: 49

    Purse total dimensions: 2 1/8" x 7 3/8 "
        Bag: 2 1/8" x 2 7/8"
        Fringe: 4 1/2"

Shadow Pony

Attach Strap

Attach Strap

Lace ▶

▲ Start Fringe

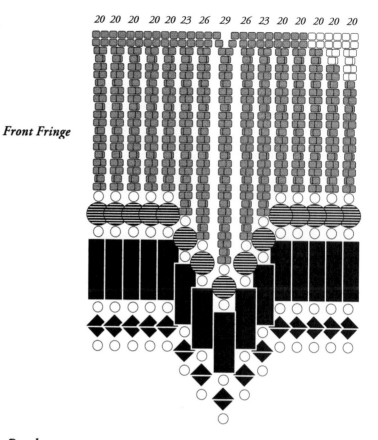

20 20 20 20 20 23 26 29 26 23 20 20 20 20 20

Front Fringe

Trim Beads

○	182 --	2 mm Sterling Silver Beads
⊖	61 --	4 mm Matte Royal Blue AB Druk Beads
⊛	19 --	4 mm Blue Lace Agate
◆	38 --	4 mm Black Austrian Crystal
▮	38 --	4 x 10 mm 5-Sided Opaque Black Beads

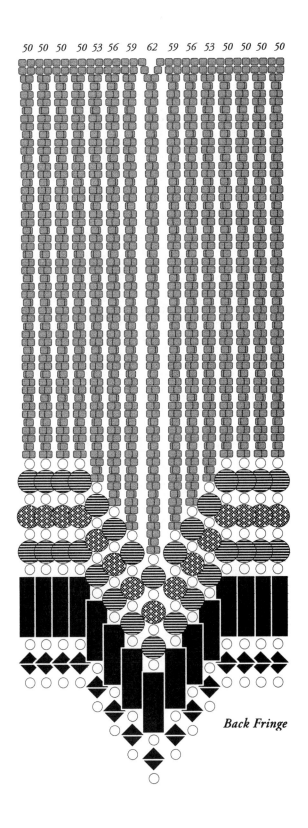

50 50 50 50 53 56 59 62 59 56 53 50 50 50 50

Back Fringe

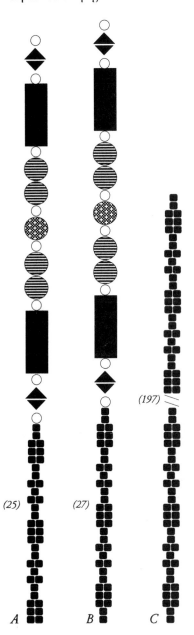

Strap
This is a variation of the
24" Peyote Style Strap
explained on page 10.

(197)

(25)   (27)

A   B   C

Peacock In India

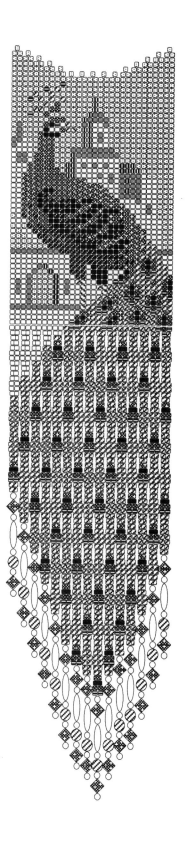

- ■ DB 25 Metallic Blue Iris
- ▨ DB 46 Silver Lined Light Green
- ▦ DB 78 Lined Aqua Mist AB
- ▨ DB 85 Lined Blue/Blue AB
- ⊗ DB 181 Silver Lined Golden Copper
- Ⓧ DB 201 White Pearl (Back - not shown)
- ▧ DB 272 Lined Topaz Yellow AB
- ▥ DB 307 Matte Metallic Grey
- ▢ DB 351 Matte White
- ▨ DB 608 Silver Lined Blue Zircon
- ▤ DB 681 Semi-Matte Silver Lined Squash AB
- ▦ DB 863 Matte Transparent Shark Grey AB

* Base Row (not shown): 53 Beads
   30 - Front Design Width
   30 - Back done in:
       DB 201 White Pearl

Total number of rows across: 30
Total rows down: 53

   Purse total dimensions: 2" x 7 3/4 "
       Bag: 2" x 3 1/4"
       Fringe: 4 4 1/2

Peacock In India

Attach Strap

Attach Strap

Lace ▶

▲ Start Fringe

© 1998 Barbara E. Elbe

Strap

This is a variation of the 24" Peyote Style Strap as shown on page 10.

33 39 45 51 57 63 67 69 73 69 65 63 57 51 45

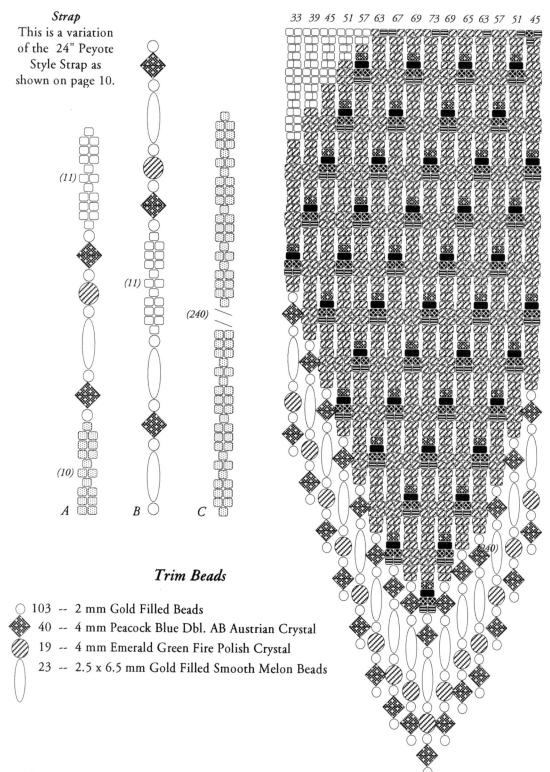

(11)

(11)

(11)

(240)

(10)

A   B   C

Trim Beads

○ 103 -- 2 mm Gold Filled Beads

◈ 40 -- 4 mm Peacock Blue Dbl. AB Austrian Crystal

◍ 19 -- 4 mm Emerald Green Fire Polish Crystal

⬭ 23 -- 2.5 x 6.5 mm Gold Filled Smooth Melon Beads

Other Titles Offered

Beaded Images *Intricate Beaded Jewelry Using Brick Stitch*
by Barbara Elbe

Contains: Sculptured parrots, peacocks and many vertical patterns. A chance to break away from the traditional brick stitch earring mold. There are sculptured Santa earrings, snowmen, candy canes and three-dimensional wreaths, Christmas trees and reindeer pins. A total of 33 unique patterns using Delica and Hexagon beads. Size 14/o seed beads can be substituted. 4 color plates, 80 pages.

Beaded Images II *Intricate Beaded Jewelry Using Brick Stitch*
by Barbara Elbe

Contains: Sculptured earring designs using horizontal and vertical base rows. Including: Horses, penguins, cats and flying mallard ducks. There are girls and clowns with three-dimensional curly hair. Bead sculpturing is fully explained (increasing and decreasing the number of beads in a row) with 29 patterns in all using Delica beads. 4 color plates, 72 pages.

Back to Beadin' *Elegant Amulet Purses & Jewelry Using Delica & Seed Beads* - by Barbara E. Elbe
    Contains: Patterns for ten beautiful amulet purses:

- Sparrow Hawk in a lake setting
- Pheasant in the woods
- Ruby-throated Hummingbird & earrings
- Bouquet in Vase & earrings
- Classic White Persian Cat & more

Eight purses done in brick stitch, one each in right angle and herringbone weave. Instructions for crocheted cord jewelry, single and double daisy chain jewelry. Completely explained and illustrated. 80 pages, plus an 8 page color insert.

Order Form

- **Supplies** – To complete any of the designs in books listed below.

- **Kits** – For all amulet purses in *Back to Beadin'* and *Amulet Obsession*.

- **Telephone Orders:**   **(530) 244-0317** – Accept **VISA** or **MasterCard ONLY**

- **FAX** 24 hours a day: **(530) 244-2336**

- **E-Mail**: BeadImages@aol.com – **Web site**: http://members.aol.com/beadimages

- **Postal Orders**: Send check or money order in US currency made payable to:

Beaded Images
556 Hanland Court
Redding, CA 96003

Beaded Images – by Barbara Elbe   _____ x $ 9.95 = _____
Beaded Images II – by Barbara Elbe   _____ x $ 9.95 = _____
Back to Beadin' – by Barbara E. Elbe   _____ x $11.95 = _____
Amulet Obsession – by Barbara E. Elbe   _____ x $13.95 = _____

CA Residents 7.25% Sales Tax   _____

Shipping: $2.25 for first book
$1.00 for each additional book   _____

TOTAL ENCLOSED   _____

Name _____

Address _____

City/State/Zip _____

Phone _____

☐ Check or Money order (in US currency)

☐ MasterCard   ☐ VISA

Credit Card #_____ - _____ - _____ - _____

Expiration Date ___/___ Cardholder's Signature _____